# Clare of Assisi

## Her Spirituality Revealed in Her Letters

Claire Marie Ledoux

Translated from the French by
Colette Joly Dees

ST. ANTHONY MESSENGER PRESS
Cincinnati, Ohio

*Imprimatur*: Daniel Labille
Bishop of Soissons, France
June 11, 1996


ISBN 2-204-05468-2
ISSN 0750-1862


ISBN 2-89420-342-X



Library of Congress Cataloging-in-Publication Data

Ledoux, Claire Marie.
Clare of Assisi : her spirituality revealed in her letters / Claire Marie Ledoux ; translated from the French by Colette Joly Dees ; preface by Yves Tourenne.
p. cm.
Includes bibliographical references.
ISBN 0-86716-368-2 (pbk.)
1. Clare, of Assisi, Saint, 1194-1253--Correspondence. 2. Christian saints--Italy--Assisi--Correspondence. 3. Spirituality--Catholic Church. I. Clare, of Assisi, Saint, 1194-1253. Correspondence. English. Selections. II. Title.
BX4700.C6 A4 2002
271'.97302--dc21

2002015710

Cover painting by Darina Gladišová,
*St. Clara Blessing Bread,* copyright ©1998
Cover design and book design by Mary Alfieri

ISBN 0-86716-368-2



Published by St. Anthony Messenger Press
www.AmericanCatholic.org

Printed in the U.S.A.

THANKS
to the Poor Clare sisters
for their confidence
and their support,
to Philippe Lécrivain, S.J.,
Germaine Lacorre,
Corinne Saveuse
and Jacques Burtin
for their valuable help
in rereading the
original manuscript
of this book.

# Contents

# Preface

This book is to be read slowly.

You will find in it Saint Clare of Assisi's life, her mission and her thought. Yet, even more than that, you will find a testimony on Jesus Christ, who reveals the secret of the invisible God and the meaning of Christianity.

Then, bearing in mind the balance of Clare's thought, described in more detail in the Conclusion, you may want to meditate on some passage of the book before returning to your daily life.

## *Methodology*

The author brings out what is implicit in the faith, the love of God and the loving service of others that filled the life of Clare of Assisi.

Clare was neither a theologian nor a philosopher. Yet, because she offered Jesus all her intelligence as a believer, she received the gift of knowing in depth the essence of human experience. Today we would say anthropology is hidden in Christology (see Colossians 2:3).

This book is made up of two parts: "The Lives of Human Beings" and "The Poor Christ." The order is important. If God was definitively and absolutely revealed in and through one man in history, Jesus of Nazareth, then Christianity must "speak" to the hearts of humans, of all men and women and even of "unimportant beings."

Therefore, in reading and rereading this introduction to Clare of Assisi, we must focus not only on the second part but also we should see why the first part is indispensable.

## *Content*

**Contemplating divine revelation.** God revealed himself to us as he is and chose to use the reality of the universe and, even more, human reality in history as the divine language for doing so. By becoming human, the Creator expressed and gave himself to his noblest creature. This is the heart of Christianity, the marvelous exchange through which God gives to human beings the gift of receiving and bringing God into the world. This is not a self-lowering of God. Instead, "in bringing us to the divine stature, God was not satisfied with adopting ours."[1]

In Clare's writings, we find images evoking the heart of Christianity. How can we speak of God without images? Only if these images are transpierced and consumed by a faith that recognizes in all things the only Lord, greater and poorer than anything we can conceive, the Word who cannot be grasped, the Word who became flesh.

First and foremost, Christianity is founded on divine revelation. Today we can emphasize its three decisive elements:

—The Infinite One does not ask us to curse or to forget our limitations. They are blessed and divinely redeemed. Christianity does not call humans to lose themselves in the vastness of the universe. God calls each one of us by name. In the eternity of the trinitarian glory, each one of us will be unique.

—Christianity is the religion of absolute gratuity: God gives freely, "much beyond our merits and our wishes."[2] But grace does not crush human beings. God grants us the gift of being, of always starting to live anew and of persevering in faith and in love. Clare lived this perseverance given by grace in her vocation to a new form of religious life.

—Human beings are fascinated by beauty. They can project this desire for beauty into a thousand forms of idolatry. But when God, in his divine intimacy, revealed himself to us, God stripped himself of glory and appeared as a man without beauty and humiliated, "the rubbish of the world"[3] among the vanquished of history. "God accepts appearing defenseless and powerless, becoming unrecognizable, invisible for the multitude of people accustomed to recognizing God only in signs of majesty and in outbursts of anger."[4] Following in Clare's footsteps, we can contemplate God's beauty in Jesus' suffering and being crucified for us. However, this contemplation is truly pious and Christian only if it draws us away from all fascination with beauty in order to transform us into ordinary servants in daily life, which is not always beautiful.

**Welcoming revelation in faith.** Clare was baptized. She was a believer. While Christianity is wholly based on the revelation of God, who gives himself freely and divinely, there can only be revelation if we can receive it as revelation and make it our own. God graces us with faith, with responding yes to the yes that God speaks to us forever. Thus, revelation welcomed in faith becomes in us an intimate knowledge of God, life under the Parent's kind gaze and the freedom of sons and daughters in the only Son.

Being both baptized and a believer, Clare can therefore "speak" to all the baptized and to all believers, not just to religious sisters. Her faith, which helped her to discern God's plan in the midst of obscure circumstances and sufferings, helps all of us believers to make of our trials stages on the long journey of becoming ourselves at last in following Jesus, "the pioneer and perfecter of our faith" (Hebrews 12:2).

Thus, faith can "realize"[5] the thanksgiving, the thanks that makes us free because the gift-giver did not impose his gifts but, rather, enabled us to make them ours, to transform them into our most personal talents: "When you crown our merits, you are crowning your own gifts."[6]

Here and now, in the day's chiaroscuro and even in the night's darkness and tears, faith gifts us with knowing intimately the One who has known us (see 1 Corinthians 13:12). At the moment of her death, Clare's faith was expressed in gratitude: "Blessed are you, Lord, You who created me!"

**Ecclesiology.** Revelation and Christian faith are impossible without the church, the "milieu" planned by God, a milieu in and through which God is already elaborating the new creation. This milieu includes God's church in Assisi, at San Damiano, but also the whole church on earth and in heaven, through the ministry of the bishop who holds the see of Rome as a sign of unity.

Clare loved the church. Yet, she was amazingly free and unswerving in discerning what was human, all too human, in the church of her time, as well as in living God's call to her to serve all the baptized.

We can see Clare's "ecclesiology" in her Rule, her Testament and in her determined attitude with regard to church demands. Clare knew the realities of the institution and the canonical structures. But the church is also the communion of saints and each baptized person lives and suffers for others.

Clare's was a discreet and living ecclesiology. On her sickbed, Clare used to spin. She had corporals, or altar cloths, made and would send them to the churches of the town and the Assisi diocese.

### *Reading Saint Clare at the Present Time*

Reading the accounts of Saint Clare's life and praying with her writings should help us to live our lives as baptized and confirmed Christians today, whether we are married or single, ordained ministers or religious or laypersons. We are at the service of the world in worshipping God and attending to God's life, just as Clare and her sisters did.

There has been a return of the use of sacred symbols in today's secular world. It is as if extreme secularism tries to make up for God's absence through an abundance of references to and use of the sacred. However, this return of the sacred is far from being a rediscovery of the God and Father of Jesus, the God whose revelation of love is expressed in the newborn of Bethlehem, the crucified one on Golgotha and in a believing people, namely, the church.

To today's world all that Christianity has to offer is that which Christianity alone can give: the revelation that, once and for all, the Infinite has embraced every human situation—even the darkest one—to make life spring forth from death. And in this revelation, all of us women, men and children can be reborn, carry our crosses with Jesus and become active and fruitful members of the human community and of the church, though we remain marked by suffering or by sin.

## *Opening*

I give thanks to the Author of grace.[7]
*—Clare*

I would have liked for a God to exist.
I long to praise him and to thank him.[8]
*—Katherine Mansfield*

In 1923, toward the end of her life, a fairly young woman joined a theosophic community in Avon, near Fontainebleau in France.

For a long time she had been searching for the secret of the world, sensing that the least human being was upheld by a primordial grace and simplicity.

She knew how to look at reality through a pure heart. "I am always on the verge of giving my blessing to what I contemplate," she said.[9]

This woman, Katherine Mansfield, sensed that there is an unknown at the heart of reality and that it is a joy to surrender to this unknown by welcoming others. She used to say that "suffering has to become Love."[10]

After she had burned her bridges, she wanted to discover the real life she had always sought in an esoteric community totally outside of Christianity. And yet, on March 29, 1922, she had written: "But the more I study the religion of Christ, the more it amazes me."[11] However, after having stopped her writing of fiction, these words, written a few days before her death, express the purity and the limit of her quest: "If I could raise a single clamor to God, you see, it would be: I want to be REAL."[12]

From one woman to another, from Clare of Assisi to Katherine Mansfield, we see a similar search for real life, the gift of a pure look at reality. But in Jesus Christ, Clare recognized the source and the goal of her quest, "the joy prepared for us beyond all our imagining."[13]

May Saint Clare help us to live and bear witness to the One who came to give us life in abundance, the One who is giving himself today in the Word, the sacraments and the community of the church.

Brother Yves Tourenne, O.F.M.
*April 29, 1996, on the*
*Feast of Saint Catherine of Siena*

## *Notes*

[1] Maurice Blondel, *Annales*, July 1907, from Maurice Blondel and Lucien Laberthonnière, *Correspondance philosophique*, presented by Claude Tresmontant (Paris: Editions du Seuil, 1961), p. 207.

[2] Opening prayer of the Twenty-seventh Sunday in Ordinary Time.

[3] 1 Corinthians 4:13. Paul means that, through his apostolic experience, he participates in the divine revelation of God in the passion and the crucifixion of Jesus.

[4] Joseph Moingt, S.J., *L'homme qui venait de Dieu* (Paris: Editions du Cerf, coll. "Cogitatio Fidei," 1993), p. 542.

[5] That is, "intimately understand and accomplish in depth."

[6] Preface of saints of Augustinian inspiration.

[7] 2 LAg 3.

[8] Quotation from André Blanchet, "Le secret de Katherine Mansfield," in *La Littérature et le Spirituel*, vol. 3 (Paris: Aubier), p. 112. See also Gabriel Marcel in the preface he wrote for the translation of Katherine's *Letters* (Paris: Stock, 1931). Katherine Mansfield was born in 1888 in New Zealand. She died in 1923 in Avon, near Fontainebleau, France. A writer, she left us admirable short stories. In some aspects, she was close to Chekhov but also to Rimbaud and Nietzsche.

[9] Blanchet, p. 103.

[10] *Ibid.*, p. 106.

[11] Marcel, p. 311.

[12] Written in upper case in the text. *Ibid.*, p. 342; letter from Avon, December 26, 1922.

[13] Opening prayer of the Twentieth Sunday in Ordinary Time.

# List of Abbreviations Used in this Text

| | |
|---|---|
| 1 LAg | First letter to Agnes of Prague |
| 2 LAg | Second letter to Agnes of Prague |
| 3 LAg | Third letter to Agnes of Prague |
| 4 LAg | Fourth letter to Agnes of Prague |
| RCl | Rule |
| TestCl | Testament |
| BCl | Clare's Blessing |
| 1 PrPov | The Privilege of Poverty of Pope Innocent III (1216) |
| 2 PrPov | The Privilege of Poverty of Pope Gregory IX (1228) |
| ECl | *Ecrits* (Paris: Editions du Cerf, Coll. "Sources chrétiennes," no. 325, 1985). |
| ED | *Clare of Assisi: Early Documents*, edited and translated by Regis J. Armstrong, O.F.M. CAP. |

Unless otherwise noted, the quotations from the texts of Clare of Assisi come from *Clare of Assisi: Early Documents, Revised and Expanded*, edited and translated by Regis J. Armstrong, O.F.M. CAP. (St. Bonaventure, N.Y.: Franciscan Institute Publications, 1993).

# Chronology

1181 (or 1182): Birth of John di Pietro di Bernardone, called Francis

1193 (or 1194): Birth of Clare di Favarone di Offreduccio

1205: Start of Francis' conversion

1210–1212: Clare meets Francis.

1212 Palm Sunday: Clare receives the religious habit from the hands of Francis at the Portiuncula. — Clare stays at the monastery of San Paolo delle Abbadesse in Bastia and at the Church of Sant'Angelo in Panzo. —April 3–4: Clare's sister Agnes joins her. —End of April–start of May: Clare settles at San Damiano.

1212–1215: Francis gives "Form of Life" to Clare and her companions (RCl 6, 3-4).

1215: Clare adopts the Rule of Saint Benedict and she is given the title of abbess. Privilege of poverty granted by Pope Innocent III for San Damiano Monastery

1216: Pope Honorius III succeeds Innocent III.

1219: Rule of Cardinal Hugolino

1224: Francis receives the stigmata. Beginning of Clare's illness

1225: March–May: Francis, who is almost blind, stays at San Damiano Monastery, where he writes the *Canticle of Creatures*.

1226: Ortolana (Clare's mother) enters San Damiano Monastery. —End of September–start of October: Francis makes final recommendations to Clare and her sisters (RCl 6, 6–9) —October 3: Francis' death

1227: Gregory IX (former Cardinal Hugolino), pope

1228 July 16: Canonization of Francis by Pope Gregory IX —September 17: Gregory IX renews the privilege of poverty.

1228 or 1229: Clare's sister Agnes becomes abbess at the Monticelli Monastery

1229: Clare's sister Beatrice enters San Damiano.

1234: Clare's first letter to Agnes of Prague (prior to Agnes' entering the Prague Monastery)

1234–1238: Clare's second letter to Agnes of Prague

1238: Clare's third letter to Agnes of Prague

1240 September: Invasion of San Damiano Monastery by the Saracens

1241: Celestine IV, pope. Innocent IV succeeds him.

1247 August 6: Rule of Innocent IV for the Order of San Damiano. Clare starts to write her own Rule.

1250 Around November 11: Clare's illness gets worse.

1253: Clare's fourth letter to Agnes of Prague —April 27: Innocent IV visits Clare for the first time. —Shortly before August 11, 1253: Innocent IV visits Clare for the second time. —August 9: Innocent IV approves Clare's Rule. —August 11: Clare's death —October 18: Innocent IV instructs Bartholomew of Spoleto to investigate Clare's life and miracles. —November 24–29: Process of Clare's canonization

1254: Alexander IV, pope

1255 August 15: Clare's canonization by Alexander IV, in Anagni

1893: Discovery of the original bull containing Clare's Rule

# Introduction

How can it be that such an amazing and rich personality as Clare of Assisi has not awakened more interest? Founder with Francis of Assisi of a new order, the Poor Sisters or Poor Clares, not only is Clare the first woman in the history of the church to have written a Rule for women, but she is also the author of remarkable spiritual writings. Only a small part of these texts has come to us. This is not because Clare did not write much but, rather, because little attention was paid to her writings. Either her writing was ignored or it was not fully appreciated.[1]

Clare must delight in being ignored or unknown by many today. As a matter of fact, throughout her life Clare sought self-effacement in the privacy of her monastery. She led a humble and poor life of service and monotony, tempered by unexpected illness, trials and temptations. Clare played an important role in the spiritual journey of Francis of Assisi. Yet, throughout literature, she seems to have disappeared behind the figure of the little poor man of Assisi.[2] At best, Clare is seen as a feminine variant of the evangelical intuition of Francis.

However, a very different image of Clare emerges from her writings. We perceive in them a determined, combative and persevering feminine personality with infinite patience. Clare used stubborn diplomacy in order to carry out her plan. She assumed responsibility for the steps necessary to assure the success of what she valued above all else: to live the gospel in following Jesus Christ while remaining close to Francis and the Order and remaining faithful to the church. Obviously, this fidelity was not without suffering. But Clare probably prefers that this suffering remain hidden. What is important for her is that we bear witness to her happiness in "following Christ,"[3] an attitude that prevailed throughout her life.

This work is not presented as a biography of Clare of Assisi. *Clare of Assisi* attempts merely to bring out of the shadows—where centuries have kept them hidden—a few essential aspects of Clare's spirituality and her thinking about Jesus Christ and human beings.

Following a brief look at the major events of Clare's life, this book includes two major parts. Part One, "The Lives of Human Beings," seeks to understand who we are in Clare's thinking. Part Two, "The Poor Christ," attempts to answer the question: Who is Jesus Christ for Clare?

Despite their different forms, as a whole, Clare's writings show a deep unity of thought. In her Rule Clare outlines what is literally the heart of her "Form of Life,"[4] that is, the fundamental evangelical elements about which she was uncompromising. This document clarifies and fully expresses what she meant by "to live according to the perfection of the holy Gospel" (RCl 6, 3).

In her Testament Clare recalls her beginnings and some important points of her life according to the gospel. She underscores, above all, the special character of her foundation, that is, her attachment to the "Form of Life" that Francis left her and which she carefully included in the very heart of her Rule (RCl 6).

Clare's Blessing is closely related to the conclusion of her Testament, continuing it in liturgical terms.

Among the writings as a whole, Clare's letters to Agnes of Prague[5] come closest to being a treatise on spiritual life. Thus, we have chosen to include here a detailed reading of these letters. Our goal has been to discover the core of Clare's spiritual and mystical experience.

The letters to Agnes do not aim at moral guidance. Instead, they establish Christian life on the mystery of the "poor Christ." The mystery of God, revealed in Jesus

Christ, occupies an essential place. We cannot separate human beings from God. Created in God's image, of all creatures we are the most worthy, greater than heaven, since the Creator, whom the heavens could not contain, came to dwell in humankind (3 LAg 21, 22). Yet, this positive and optimistic image of human beings is grounded in realism. Clare knows that we are weak and frail and fundamentally proud, an attitude that is often expressed in our deep-seated desire to possess and dominate.

Clare of Assisi never intended to write a theological work. We find no doctrinal treatise in what she wrote. However, her letters to Agnes of Prague contain a wealth that we are just beginning to explore. These texts reveal a rich and strong vision of human beings and of God. Brother Thaddée Matura aptly says of them, "What occupies the first place in these Writings, as in all spiritual works, is a certain way of seeing God and the relationships that humans can establish with God's mystery."[6]

## *Notes*

[1] Even in Franciscan circles, knowledge of Clare's writings only became widespread after 1925, and only recently did we start to analyze their content. Although there were several editions of Clare's works from 1930 to 1970, we can emphasize that the edition of these texts in their original Latin, along with a French translation, was published for the first time in 1985 in the collection "Sources chrétiennes." Note: There is no similar edition (Latin text, plus translation) in English. The first English translation of Clare's writings was published by Ignatius Brady, O.F.M., and Mary Francis, S.M.I.C., *The Legend and Writings of Saint Clare of Assisi*, St. Bonaventure University, 1953. It was based on the German publication by Engelbert Grau, O.F.M., *Leben und Schriften der heiligen Klara von Assisi* (Werl/Westfalen, 1952).

[2] The nickname given to Saint Francis of Assisi.

[3] Thomas of Celano, "The Legend Saint Clare," 1, 14, ED. The complete references of the quoted works are given in the Bibliography, pp. 123.

[4] RCl 1, 1. Clare never uses the word "Rule." Instead, she uses "Form of Life." However, to provide a better understanding, we have chosen to use this first expression.

[5] Agnes of Prague (1205–1282) was the daughter of King Ottokar I of Bohemia (1197–1230) and of Queen Constance of Hungary. When she was three, Agnes was engaged to Boleslav of Silesia (d. 1211), then in 1213, to the son of Emperor Frederick II, Henry, two years old at the time. After the engagement was broken in 1225, King Henry III of England asked for Agnes's hand in 1227, then Frederick II himself asked in 1228 and again in 1233. But this was not to be Agnes's destiny. She freely chose to follow the religious life instituted by Clare and Francis of Assisi.

[6] Thaddée Matura, Introduction, chapter II, "Trois centres d'intérêt," c. "La douceur que ressentent les amis" in: ECl, p. 52. There is no published English translation of this work.

## The Life of Clare of Assisi

One would like to know who Clare was and the type of life she led in the narrow confines of her little monastery. One would like to be able to follow Clare in her years of intellectual and spiritual formation, first in the shadow of her family and later in San Damiano. One would like to know not only the name of Francis of Assisi but also the names of the men and women who taught her to interpret the gospel and to pray.

Clare's life unfolded entirely inside the tiny area of Assisi, so it is right that her name is closely linked to that of her city. Therefore, in order to grasp the fundamental aspects of her existence, we must briefly mention a few facts about the social and political life of this small Umbrian city where Clare was born and where she always lived.

### *Asissi at the End of the Twelfth Century*

At the end of the twelfth century, in the heart of central Italy, Assisi was famous for its political rifts. In 962, Otto,[1] the King of Germany, was crowned emperor of the Holy Roman Empire by Pope John XII. Shortly after that, a lengthy struggle opposed the empire and the papacy in an attempt to reduce the Germanic emperor's political and temporal powers. When Clare was born in Assisi in 1193, Frederick Barbarossa[2] ruled, having conquered the city sixteen years earlier. The Rocca Maggiore, a fortress that stands above the city of Assisi where Conrad of Urslingen[3] had established himself, symbolizes this painful event.

A new power was soon to rise up. At that time, most of the cities of Italy were subject to feudal lords. The cities were the property of an abbot, a bishop or a count. The emergence and rapid development of an urban world, increasingly dominated by a newly emerging middle class of merchants, constituted an authentic revolution in the heart of feudal and rural society. A new world was being established in the old one and, with it, bringing the inversion of every custom. In some places, merchants had obtained considerable economic privileges from the feudal lords. Once they had economic freedom, merchants quickly aspired to political freedom and claimed the right to administer their own assets. They formed guilds or communes to achieve these goals. This marked the birth of the guild movement, which spread rapidly to all of Europe with the goal of freeing every city from feudal power.[4]

As a result of all these changes, material poverty was increasing. Communes had impoverished serfs by fighting the lords to take away their fiefs, leaving the serfs without livelihood. Extreme poverty was increasing in cities. The wealth of some merchants contrasted with the people's growing poverty. Poverty began to become a real social problem. This increasingly more visible destitution disturbed Christian consciences and secular society. In cities pious confraternities emerged. They built hospices for the poor and the sick and, in many cases, they became hospitaller communities. Works of mercy developed and charitable institutions responded to society's need during this period of urban expansion and rapid population growth.

### *The World in 1193*

There was change and turmoil beyond the borders of Assisi as well. Since 1187 Jerusalem had been in the hands of Saladin.[5] Once again, the pope encouraged crusades. For Christians the thought of Christ's tomb being in the hands of those outside the church had become intolerable.

When Innocent III was elected pope on January 8, 1198, the church itself appeared to be considerably weakened, to the point that new evangelical movements emerged. Like those of previous centuries, they proposed a return to the early church. Opposing the political and religious system of church seigniories (feudal territories held by the church) and holy wars, these various movements mingled with the famous Cathari,[6] Waldenses,[7] Patarines[8] and other movements. They all sought to return to the gospel of poverty, brotherhood and peace.

It is in this social context, rich in human aspirations and full of contradictions, that we consider the life of Clare of Assisi.

### *Clare's Youth*

Clare was born in 1193 or 1194. It is difficult to be more specific about the date. Her family belonged to the local nobility of Assisi. Her parents, Ortolana and Favarone di Offreduccio di Bernardo, lived in an important area of the city where the most illustrious families lived. Her birth was relatively unnoticed in a family whose nobility did not draw attention to itself by great deeds.

Does that mean that Clare was just like any other little girl? Not exactly, since as a child she had the capacity to amaze people around her. At the school of Ortolana's charitable works, Clare strove to imitate her mother. The clamor of the poor, who were dying of hunger, rose to the doors of her house and Clare heard it. Assisi was going through a period of desolation and misery, sadly known as the "deadly hunger." Her first biographer, Thomas of Celano,[9] gives us the best description of life in Clare's house. He writes,

> She freely stretched out her hand to the poor (Proverbs 31:20) and satisfied the needs of many out of the abundance of her house (2 Corinthians 8:14). In order that her sacrifice would be more pleasing to

> God, she would deprive her own body of delicate foods and, sending them secretly through intermediaries, she would nourish the bodies of the poor (Job 31:17).[10]

Thus, Clare embraced the world of the poor who came begging at the door of the family home. As she became more sensitive to their distress, she made a bewildering discovery: when she found herself alone, her heavy heart was filled with compassion for the poor, and she raised her eyes toward another poor one, the crucified Jesus. God's humanity was revealed to her in the faces of the destitute. Clare's entire spiritual journey to Christ is rooted in a life of solidarity and sharing with Assisi's most deprived people. There is complete identification for Clare of the beggar at the door of her house and the "poor Christ" who had become the least among humans.

### *Francis' Conversion*

At the beginning of his Testament when Francis mentioned the decisive stage of his conversion, he recalled his essential encounter with lepers:

> The Lord gave me, Brother Francis, thus to begin doing penance in this way: for when I was in sin, it seemed too bitter for me to see lepers. And the Lord Himself led me among them and I showed mercy to them. And when I left them, what had seemed bitter to me was turned into sweetness of soul and body. And afterwards I delayed a little and left the world.[11]

Francis' conversion is linked with a very definite and concrete experience: his encounter with the misery of his time represented by the disfigured faces of lepers. The son of a wealthy merchant of Assisi, Francis became aware that the world in which he became an adult was not ruled by brotherhood and solidarity but, rather, by the prestige of wealth and the exploitation of the weak by the rich.

When he wrote in his Testament: "I delayed a little and left the world," Francis had in mind the concrete, definite and structured world of Assisi. In the presence of lepers expelled from society, Francis made the free and conscious decision to abandon the world of Assisi to start his project of living among the excluded. He discovered the gospel when he set his eyes on the poor and allowed them to challenge him with their questions.

Life in Assisi appeared to Francis to mean being gripped in the jaws of political power and under the domination of wealth. In order to live the gospel, to follow in the footsteps of Jesus, Francis needed to be at a certain distance from Assisi's society. However, this distance did not mean a flight from the world. Francis' life became rooted in the gospel, in the history of the life of Jesus and his dying on the cross for the redemption of men and women. The person of Jesus became the center of Francis' life and Jesus sent him directly back to the world of people. Francis became aware of two realities: on one hand, the world is the place where God is at work (it is God's creation), but, on the other hand, the world is also the place where people are free to encounter and to deny God. This twofold feeling penetrated deeply into Francis' heart.

At the time of his conversion, Francis did not intend to found an order but, rather, to really live the gospel. However, very quickly he had brothers, then sisters (Clare and her sisters) and later, more laypeople who, while they remained single or married, were converted to his example.[12] These people, who were from different social groups, wanted to share Francis' way of finding fulfillment and meaning for their lives. They discovered a way of living the gospel very close to that of the Christians of the early church, a way characterized primarily by the harmony between being and doing. They understood that in order to proclaim the Good News to the poor, cleanse lepers and heal the sick, they had to be close to the poor by being poor themselves and by being satisfied with the bare necessities of clothing and food.

### *Clare Meets Francis*

During the years 1206 to 1212, Clare was struck by Francis' choice of poverty. The dramatic intensity of his radical conversion impressed her. For Clare, Francis' life was an authentic gospel word, revealing God's face to her and inviting her to follow Jesus Christ in poverty and joy. This is the way Thomas of Celano relates the memory of these first encounters between Clare and Francis:

> [Francis] visited her and she more frequently him, moderating the times of their visits so that this divine pursuit could not be perceived by anyone nor objected to by gossip. For, with only one close companion accompanying her, the young girl, leaving her paternal home, frequented the clandestine meetings with the man of God, whose words seemed to her to be on fire and whose deeds were seen to be beyond the human.[13]

A great and beautiful friendship between Francis and Clare started this way. Francis spoke to her about the gospel, about the burning Word that set his heart on fire, and, hearing Francis' preaching, Clare soon took steps to serve God. She sold her inheritance and gave the money to the poor, according to the word of the Gospel: ". . . go, sell your possessions, and give the money to the poor, and you will have treasure in heaven; then come, follow me" (Matthew 19:21; cf. RCl 2, 7).

Clare made a radical break with her social class by choosing to dispose of her inheritance in this way. She refused the wealth, glory and prestige of nobility. Not only did she give her assets to the poor but she herself became poor. From then on, her opting for poverty set her up against the noble class of her lineage. From the time of her conversion, poverty became and would remain for Clare a way of life, the indispensable foundation for realizing her religious ideal. By her choice to live in poverty, like Francis, although in her own original way, Clare was challenging a society in which strength, power and money were masters and in which the church itself was the empire's rival power.

### *A Singular Way of Receiving the Habit*

On the night of Palm Sunday, 1212, Clare secretly left her family home to go to a little church in the Assisi plain, the Portiuncula.[14] There, welcomed by the brothers watching in prayer around the altar, Clare received from Francis a poor habit like his own and had her hair cut as a sign of her consecration to God—a singular way indeed of receiving the habit. Francis did not follow the customs of his time! On this subject, Marco Bartoli writes:

> Clare was not an ordinary young girl leaving her parents to enter monastic life; rather she was a young woman who had run away from home, going forth to meet contempt and disapproval from everyone. Nor was Francis a bishop—to whom the consecration of virgins was normally reserved. In fact, he was not even a priest but only a layman, and yet he took upon himself the right to consecrate Clare to the Lord.[15]

By taking this task upon himself, Francis created a precedent: to assume directly the responsibility for a new form of religious life. Clare could not simply share the life of Francis and his brothers just as it was. Marco Bartoli reports:

> Obviously a friendship between the Poverello and the eldest daughter of one of the main families in the city could have given rise to comments which would have been far from kindly, especially in Assisi where public reputation was so important. Francis, on any number of occasions, had shown that he himself

> cared nothing for either the risk or the reality of a negative judgment by the crowd, but it is more than likely that he was worried by Clare's request. A woman wanting to share his way of life was certainly no small problem: how could she share the poverty and mendicancy of the Poverello and his first companions? About ten years later when he was putting his Rule into writing, Francis warns his brethren not to receive women into the fraternity: "Absolutely no woman should be received to obedience by any brothers, but once she has been given spiritual advice, let her perform a penance where she will."[16]

For Francis, accepting women within the fraternity opened the door to many problems.[17]

In Francis' Rule, various injunctions on the subject undoubtedly came from the experience of the first years of the Franciscan community. They seem to "have been a component of Franciscan spirituality right from the start. The responsibilities of his choice actually imposed upon Francis an attitude toward chastity which was every bit as radical as his attitudes to poverty and obedience."[18]

After her welcoming at the Portiuncula, Francis led Clare to the Benedictines of the Monastery of San Paolo delle Abbadesse about four miles from Assisi. Clare stayed there only a few days and then went on to the church of Sant'Angelo in Panzo, where her sister Agnes joined her. A group of religious women (probably Beguines) were living near this church, located above Assisi on the slopes of Mount Subasio. This is what Marco Bartoli relates:

> [W]hen Clare went to that little church on the slopes of Subasio, what did she find there? It is impossible to give an exact answer. Certainly it was by no means unknown for a woman who wanted to live an intense life of prayer and penance to choose to retire near a church, generally in the city although sometimes in the country nearby. There she would be supported by alms from the passers-by. In central Italy

in those years, and especially in Umbria, this was a widespread phenomenon. The first half of the thirteenth century saw a great demand for religious life on the part of women who did not find sufficient outlets through the traditional monastic channels. As a result, they fostered a whole series of new experiments. There was a similar phenomenon at the same time in other parts of Europe, especially in Brabant and around the Rhine. Here there was an upsurging of experiences of prayer, of love and the life of penance which were to come to their full flowering in the great Beguinages of northern Europe.

Probably when Clare arrived at Sant'Angelo in Panzo she found there a small group of women, leading a life of penance together but without professing any officially recognized Rule (as it is thought that the group did who later lived there). In any case, her stay at Sant'Angelo in Panzo was, for Clare, a period of making contact with the new forms of religious life which other women than herself were also striving to realize at that time.[19]

### *Foundation of San Damiano Monastery*

After leaving Sant'Angelo in Panzo, on Francis' advice, Clare and her sister Agnes decided to settle in the small church of San Damiano in the Assisi plain. Francis himself had restored it.

Many women who wanted to share the ideal of Clare and Agnes started to gather around them in San Damiano: Beatrice, another of Clare's sisters, and also her own mother, Ortolana, as well as some of the family servants. Francis wrote a "Form of Life" for these Poor Sisters, as they were first called (RCl 1,1), or for the Poor Clares, as they are called now. Later on, Clare included it at the center of her Rule. This is what Francis wrote:

> I, little brother Francis, wish to follow the life and poverty of our most high Lord Jesus Christ and of

> His holy mother and to persevere in this until the end; . . . and I ask and counsel you, my ladies, to live always in this most holy life and poverty. And keep most careful watch that you never depart from this by reason of the teaching or advice of anyone. (RCl 6, 7–9)

Here we have a fundamental attitude with a mysterious significance: we should not seek God where the rich and the powerful have the last word but, rather, in what is poor, small, humble and weak. Jesus is the one who took on "the true flesh of our humanity and of our weakness,"[20] the woes of our existence subject to poverty, evil and death. Clare and Francis understood that Jesus-like poverty and humility spring from a different way of living in the world. By choosing to live in poverty to announce the Good News of the poor Jesus, like Jesus, their only option is to go down into the depths of the human condition.

### *Daily Life at San Damiano*

We have very few details of Clare's life at San Damiano, except knowledge of the separation and silence she shared with her sisters. This simple life of deprivation made them available and open to encounter God. As Poor Sisters, they wanted the Spirit of the gospel to permeate them completely as individuals and as a community. Not only did they consecrate their lives to God, they also sought to be conformed to Christ by imitating him.

The location of San Damiano, to which Clare and her sisters withdrew, is especially significant in indicating their radical desire to follow the "poor Christ." The church of San Damiano is outside Assisi's walls, where outcasts remained—outside the protection of the city. Clare and her sisters lived in this place, along with the destitute, the transients, the homeless and, a little farther on, the lepers, those who were faceless and nameless for the residents of Assisi. Because it is outside the city walls, the small San

Damiano Monastery is less than secure, and Clare and her sisters chose this less than secure place to live. They wore simple clothing and their activities were those of the humble and modest people surrounding them. They worked the land and performed the mundane chores of daily life. They tried to befriend everyone and thereby formed new relationships.

Through their neighborly and friendly behavior, Clare and her sisters offered the testimony of a loving community that radiated beyond the confines of the monastery. Through their way of life and the place where they settled, they entered into the history and the way of life of the poor. There was seemingly nothing spectacular in their existence. Yet through it, a new way of religious life and of interpersonal relationships was made possible.

## *The Privilege of Poverty*

From then on, Clare and her sisters began an evolving penitential life, soon to be shaped by a style and a Rule, never experienced before. Whereas many religious communities of that time appealed to the supreme pontiff to obtain more privileges and new possessions, by contrast, Clare asked for the right to have no privileges, to live like most of the poor and the peasants who were totally deprived of privileges. Clare struggled for forty years to obtain the right to follow the Franciscan way of life with her sisters. In fact, at that time, it was neither customary nor in keeping with canonical law for a religious community without property to be approved by the church. Moreover, the church felt that it had to impose the Benedictine way of life—the only one known then—on Clare and her sisters.

Not only did Clare renounce receiving privileges, she explicitly asked the pope for the privilege of having no privilege at all except for the privilege of poverty. This was undoubtedly the heart of Clare's human and religious experience. In 1216, she asked Pope Innocent III for the privilege to own nothing, either personally or as a community.

> This magnificent man, congratulating such great fervor in the virgin, spoke of the uniqueness of her proposal since such a privilege had never been made by the Apostolic See. The Pope himself with great joy wrote with his own hand the first draft of the privilege [that was] sought after, so that an unusual favor might smile upon an unusual request.[21]

Thus Clare received from Innocent III the privilege of poverty, the first official apostolic document of the Franciscan Order. Clare and her sisters had only been settled in San Damiano for four years when the church granted this privilege that established them in total evangelical trust. In this document (1 PrPov 3), the pope uses expressions from Clare herself: "Because of this, *since you have sold all things and given them to the poor* (cf. Luke 18:22), you propose not to have any possessions whatsoever, clinging in all things to the footprints of Him, *the Way, the Truth, and the Life*."[22]

In 1228, after having resisted such a request, the new pope, Gregory IX, also had to give in to Clare's evangelical obstinacy and, in a second statement, he himself confirmed the privilege of poverty (2 PrPov 3).

## *Clare's Rule*

After the decision of the Fourth Lateran Council (1215) not to authorize new rules, Pope Gregory IX in 1218 and Pope Innocent IV in 1247 promulgated for Clare and her sisters Rules that contradicted their ideal of poverty. Extremely strict, these Rules were based on the Rule of Benedict.

Finally, Clare herself wrote her own Rule from 1247 to 1253. In fact, although she took some elements from the texts of Benedict, Gregory IX and Innocent IV, she drew most of her inspiration from the Rule of Saint Francis. With the strength of her source and her spiritual experience,

Clare devised an original and very personal project. Clare's Rule is now at the Protomonastery of the Poor Clares in Assisi. (However, there was no trace of it for centuries. It was only rediscovered in 1893, hidden in the folds of one of Saint Clare's garments.)

## *Clare's Lengthy Illness*

In 1224, the year in which Francis received the stigmata of the Lord's passion, Clare contracted an illness[23] that forced her to be permanently bedridden. On the subject, Thomas of Celano wrote, "during the twenty-eight years of her prolonged sickness, 'she did not murmur or utter a complaint' but holy comments and thanksgiving always came from her mouth."[24]

At the canonization process, Sister Cecilia, who shared the lives of Clare and her sisters, gave this testimony: "Clare, never wanting to be idle at any time, even during the time of her last illness, made herself rise, sit up in bed and spin. The soft cloth made by her spinning she used to make corporals and the cases to hold them, covered with silk or precious cloth. She sent them to the churches of the Assisi diocese."[25]

During her illness, Clare showed a remarkable fervor for the sacraments and especially for the Eucharist. The deliverance of San Damiano Monastery, besieged by the Saracens in 1240, was attributed to Clare's prayer. It was said that through her prayer, Assisi also was spared during the invasion of the soldiers of Emperor Frederick II in 1241.[26]

## *Clare's Death and Canonization*

Clare confronted her illness in communion with "the poor and the humble Christ" in a life of prayer and poverty. To that life, until her death, she consecrated all her passion, all her energy and all her human talents, despite the exhaustion caused by twenty-eight years of suffering failing health. The most eminent church prelates admired her and showed her kindness and trust. In the years 1227 to 1228, Pope Gregory IX wrote to her: "In the midst of the countless concerns of our pontificate and the anguish constantly oppressing our heart, you are our consolation and our joy."[27]

Clare's reputation of sanctity spread among the people and in the church: "It was finally seen that she was laboring for many days in her last agony during which the faith of the neighboring regions and the devotion of the peoples increased. She was honored daily as a real saint by the frequent visits of prelates and even cardinals."[28]

At the time of her death, Pope Innocent IV came to her bedside: "Lord Innocent IV of happy memory together with the cardinals hurried to visit the servant of Christ. Since he considered her life to be beyond that of the women of our time, he did not hesitate to honor her death with the papal presence."[29]

On August 11, 1253, Clare died as she saw "the King of glory" coming to her, and "turning towards herself, [Clare] silently addressed her soul. 'Go without anxiety,' she said, 'for you have a good escort for your journey. Go,' she said, 'for He Who created you has made you holy. And, always protecting you as a mother her child, He has loved you with a tender love. May you be blessed, O Lord,' she said, 'You Who have created my soul!"

A sister asked her to whom she was speaking. Clare answered, "I am speaking to my blessed soul." Her guide for the journey was very close. In fact, turning to one of her daughters, Clare said to her, "Do you see, O child, the King of glory Whom I see?"[30]

Very soon after Clare's death, Innocent IV ordered the start of the canonization process, and Pope Alexander IV proclaimed Clare's sanctity in the autumn of 1255, by the bull *Clara claris*.[31]

### *Expansion of the Order in the Thirteenth Century*

The Order of the Poor Sisters[32] expanded very fast. In 1228, a letter from Cardinal Raynald mentions the existence of twenty-three monasteries. As in the first years of Clare's conversion, communities were already multiplying through the initiatives of young ladies of noble families. Happy to honor the Lord, these women were building monasteries to which they themselves often withdrew. This was the case of Agnes of Prague (1234). In Olomouc, in Moravia, there was the foundation of blessed Kunigunde, daughter of King Bela IV of Hungary (1242); in 1245, in Zawiercie, in Poland, that of blessed Salomea, a Polish princess and the wife of the king of Galicia, now part of Poland; in 1234, in Saragossa, in Spain, a monastery was built on the initiative of the noble lady, Ermesende de Celles.

In 1259, Saint Louis's sister, Isabelle of France, founded a monastery in Longchamp, near Paris: the Convent of the Humility of Our Lady, soon to be called the Royal Abbey of Longchamp. With the help of five Franciscan theologians, including Saint Bonaventure, Isabelle, drawing inspiration from Clare's Rule, took care to provide her monastery with its own statutes. In 1259, the pope approved the Rule for the Royal Abbey of Longchamp.

Thus, the thirteenth century saw the rise of communities that claimed this new evangelical life. Some communities originated through small groups of penitent women, as was the case of Ermentrude in Bruges between 1210 and 1280. The friars' itinerant preaching gave rise to several foundations. New monasteries emerged in many Italian cities, near Florence, in Lombardy and in the Abruzzi. Outside Italy, the Rheims' foundation (1215) was the first in France during Clare's lifetime. Many other communities followed.

### *Fifteenth to the Twentieth Centuries*

At the start of the fifteenth century, there were over 15,000 Poor Clares living in about 400 monasteries. When the evangelical momentum slackened in the course of the centuries, reforms restored Clare's way of life. This was the case of the reform of Colette of Corbie in France[33] and of the Observant Reform in Italy.

From the sixteenth to the eighteenth centuries, major discoveries opened paths to the Order's expansion worldwide. The Poor Clares were in the Azores, the Canary Islands, in Madeira, then in Peru (in Cuzco in 1558, Lima in 1602), Mexico (1570), Colombia (1572) and in Chile (1582). In 1680, there were about 70,000 Poor Clares with close to 2,000 monasteries.

In the eighteenth century, the rise of a trend hostile to monastic life and the events of the French Revolution caused a wave of suppressions that started at the end of the reign of Louis XV. It became systematic in France in 1792, and shortly thereafter throughout Europe with the invasion of Napoleon's armies. A few decades later, a new era was solemnly inaugurated with the canonization of Saint Colette (May 24, 1807) during the pontificate of Pius VII. After the crisis had passed, communities were reborn in fervor and poverty two or three decades later.

The Poor Clares continued to become established throughout the world: in the United States (1878–1882), Canada (1902), North Africa (1931), Burma (1932) and in Southeast Asia (1935). The missionary thrust continues to be strong in Japan, Africa and Oceania. The communities of Latin America are mushrooming. Those of Mexico, Colombia and the Philippines are also very dynamic.

In 1993, worldwide, there were approximately 18,000 Poor Clares scattered over 1,000 monasteries throughout the world.

Thus, throughout the centuries, many women have lived according to Clare's evangelical intuition. Steadfast and courageous, Clare left in her writings the testimony of a devotion to certain values, including the life of the church, the close bond with the Order of the Friars Minor, poverty and concern for the poor, service, fraternal life and putting the gospel into practice. By her clear-sighted and optimistic approach to humankind, Clare invites us today to believe in human beings, "the most worthy of all creatures" (3 LAg 21). Her radically poor and humble life, as well as her profound insight into the mystery of Christ, help to make Clare's writings a highly valuable theological testimony.

## *Notes*

[1] Otto I the Great, king of Germania (936–973) and emperor of Germania (962–973). Son of Henry I the Fowler. With the church's support, he triumphed over the feudal lords and he dispossessed the German dukes for the benefit of his family. He imposed his authority over Lorraine in 944 and intervened in France where he supported Carolingian King Louis IV (948). His power was mostly based on the prestige he obtained by his victories over the Hungarians and the Slavs (955). He intervened in Italy where he had himself proclaimed as King of Pavia in 951, then proclaimed emperor in Rome by Pope John XII (962) during his second expedition, thus founding the Holy Roman Germanic Empire. He placed the papacy under his guardianship, deposed John XII in 963, then Benedict V in 964.

[2] Frederick I Barbarossa, from the Hohenstaufen family, nephew and successor of Conrad III, was Germanic emperor from 1152 to 1190.

[3] At that time, Conrad of Urslingen was responsible for the imperial rights of the city of Assisi and in charge of having the feudal laws obeyed.

[4] Eloi Leclerc, O.F.M., *François d'Assise, le retour à l'Evangile*, ch. 1, "Un changement de société," pp. 12–40. The English edition is entitled *Francis of Assisi: Return to the Gospel* (Chicago: Franciscan Herald Press, 1983).

[5] Saladin (Salah al-Din al-Ayyubi), the Ayyubid sultan of Egypt (1171–1193) and of Syria (1174-1193), seized Jerusalem (1187) and occupied most of the Frank territories (1188). These events gave rise to the third crusade. Philip Augustus, the king of France and Richard the Lion-Hearted, king of England, concentrated their

efforts on the siege of Acre. Saladin tried in vain to relieve the city. In the end, Acre fell (1191). A peace treaty was signed, leaving Syria and interior Palestine to Saladin and most of the coastal area to the Franks (1192).

[6] The Cathari (in Greek, *catharos* means "pure") were a neo-Manichaean sect widespread from the eleventh to the twelfth centuries in Lombardy, central Italy, Rhineland, Catalonia, Champagne, Burgundy and above all in Southern France (Albi, Toulouse, Carcassonne).

[7] Members of a dissident sect of the Catholic Church founded at the end of the twelfth century by Peter Valdes. In 1170, he had launched a movement called "the Poor of Lyons." Their doctrine, approved at first by the Catholic Church, was finally condemned at the Lateran Council (1179). Excommunicated, the Waldenses broke away from the church and were considered to be heretics.

[8] Pataria was a Milanese and Lombard religious movement (around 1055–1075). Its members (the Patarines) fought the wealth of the high clergy along the lines of the Gregorian reform (Gregory VII). The movement was orthodox but in the twelfth and thirteenth centuries, the followers of the popular Lombard heresies close to the Cathari were also called Patarines.

[9] While Claire Marie Ledoux attributes the writing of "The Legend of Saint Clare" to Thomas of Celano, there has been much dispute among scholars about the authorship of the work.

[10] Thomas of Celano, 1, 3, p. 254, ED.

[11] Francis of Assisi, "Testament," v. 1–3, p. 124, *Francis of Assisi: Early Documents*, Vol. I.

[12] "The Life of Saint Francis by Thomas of Celano," ch. 15, no. 37, p. 216, *Francis of Assisi: Early Documents*, Vol. I.

[13] Thomas of Celano, 1, 5, pp. 256–257, ED.

[14] This term comes from the Italian and it means "small parcel of land." The Portiuncula is the name of the first church given to Francis and his brothers at the beginning of the Order by the Benedictines of Mount Subasio (near Assisi). Later on, the Portiuncula became the Order's most traditional place where brothers, from the entire world, would meet for their yearly chapters.

[15] Marco Bartoli, *Clare of Assisi*, trans. Sister Frances Teresa, O.S.C. (Quincy, Ill.: Franciscan Press, 1993), p. 45.

[16] *Ibid.*, p. 42.

[17] Francis of Assisi, "The Earlier Rule," ch. 12, *Francis of Assisi: Early Documents*, Vol. I, pp. 72–73.

[18] Bartoli, p. 43.

[19] *Ibid.*, p. 55.

[20] "This most worthy, holy and glorious Word of the Father was sent from heaven by the most high Father through the angel Gabriel into the womb of the holy and glorious Virgin Mary. From her womb, the Word received the true flesh of our humanity and of our weakness" ("Later Admonition and Exhortation," *Francis of Assisi: Early Documents,* Vol. I, p. 45).

[21] Thomas of Celano, "The Legend of Saint Clare," I, 14, p. 269, ED.

[22] "The Privilege of Poverty of Pope Innocent III (1216), p. 86, ED; "The Privilege of Poverty of Pope Gregory IX (1228), pp. 107–108, ED.

[23] Historical sources give us few details about Clare's illness (or illnesses). Thomas of Celano only mentions that, "Since the strength of her flesh had succumbed to the austerity of the penance [she had practiced] in the early years, a harsh sickness took hold of her last years" ("The Legend of Saint Clare," 39, p. 291, ED).

[24] *Ibid.*

[25] Sister Cecilia, daughter of Gualtieri Cacciaguerra of Spoleto, "The Acts of the Process of Canonization," Sixth Witness, no. 14, p. 160, ED.

[26] Thomas of Celano, "The Legend of Saint Clare," 21–23, pp. 276–277, ED.

[27] Rev. Fr. Exupère (Exupère de Prats-de-Mollo), *L'Esprit de sainte Claire,* p. 208 (text quoted in: *Une Clarisse de Nice, Regard sur l'histoire des Clarisses,* t. 1, ch. 2, no. 4, "Quarante ans de fidélité," p. 54).

[28] Thomas of Celano, "The Legend of Saint Clare," 44, p. 294, ED.

[29] *Ibid.*, 41, p. 293.

[30] *Ibid.*, 46, p. 296.

[31] "Bull of canonization of Saint Clare," pp. 229–237.

[32] For what pertains to the extension of the Order of Saint Clare, one may refer to Sister Marie Colette of Nice (a Poor Clare of Nice), *Regard sur l'histoire des clarisses,* t. I-II-III.

[33] Saint Colette (or Nicole) was a Poor Clare (Corbie, 1381; Ghent, 1447). She lived as a recluse (1402). Then, Benedict XIII, the Avignon pope, gave her the mission to reform the three Franciscan Orders: First Order, the brothers of Saint Francis of Assisi, Second Order, the sisters of Saint Clare of Assisi and Third Order, men and women living under the Rule of Saint Francis of Assisi for laypeople.

# Some Aspects of Clare's Thought

The contemplation of the mystery of divine poverty revealed in Jesus Christ is at the heart of Clare's thought. Let us consider some of the distinguishing points of Clare's thought in order to accompany her on her journey.

## *Mystical and Theological Thought*

Clare strives repeatedly to express the mystery of the encounter between God and human beings with all the nuances of reason, language and poetry. In this sense, Clare's thought is mystical.[1]

Insofar as she expresses the dialogue of humans with the mystery of God manifested in Jesus Christ, we can also say that Clare's thought is theological,[2] because the profound dimension of her most intimate thought about God and humankind is at the heart of her mystical experience.

## *Drawing on Christian Sources*

In her mystical and theological writing, Clare does not limit herself only to experience. She is influenced by the patristic literature[3] that was known in her time, such as the works of Ambrose, Benedict, Gregory the Great and Leo the Great. Although Clare's inspiration comes from tradition, her thought draws mainly on Scripture: the Psalms, the Song of Solomon and especially the Gospels of John, Matthew and Luke, the Acts of the Apostles and Paul's letters.

It is true that frequent reference to the gospel is an aspect of the sensitivity of the period: during these effervescent Middle Ages, many groups and movements expressed a desire to return to the simplicity of the gospel and to the form of life of Jesus with his own apostles. However, with Clare, this return to the gospel goes beyond the commonly proposed ideal. Her approach is more all-encompassing: it is a question of following the gospel, that is to say, following in "the footprints of the poor and humble Jesus Christ" (3 LAg 4) and conforming all her being and all her life to him. "The Form of Life of Clare of Assisi" (RCl) is rooted in the spiritual attitude of "being" much more than with an adopted lifestyle.

### *Expressing the Dynamism of Life*

Clare's thought is dynamic because it springs from her experience of life. At times, this dynamism of life, expressed in her writing, follows the rhythm of a lively and joyful race. Filled with unexpected developments, Clare's thought can jump from considerations about people to a meditation on the life of Christ, or from reflections on the Truth[4] to a contemplation of God's mystery and back to human mystery.

### *Seeing Poverty as the Only Wealth*

One word characterizes Clare's theological thought. She repeats and constantly uses this little paradoxical word: "poverty." The fullest meaning of the word for Clare refers to the experience of Christ's poverty. This word is the keystone of her thought. It expresses the greatness of Christ's life and that of human beings, since it is in that poverty that we find our wealth. Clare is always returning to this fundamental intuition. She expresses it poetically and celebrates it with many melodies.

### *Seeing Love as a Relationship*

Born of a living encounter with God and a loving communion with human beings and with things, Clare's thought primarily evokes relationship and love. This is why her theological meditation rises to the love of God manifested in Jesus Christ. Her reflection on human beings focuses on their relationship with God and other people. Her entire vision of humans and of God is rooted in the notion of love as the authentic and spontaneous way of relational living.

## *Notes*

[1] We define "mystical" as the experience of the interior and unifying encounter of humans with the divine infinite that is the foundation of the divine being and of all existence.

[2] By "theological," we mean that the work attempts to elaborate a discourse (*logos*) on God (*theos*) or a word about God.

[3] In church history, these terms refer to dogmas and theology, the written works of the Fathers of the Church (the Doctors of the Church from the first to the fourth centuries).

[4] Clare calls Christ "the Truth" (3 LAg 23).

# Part One

# The Lives of Human Beings

## Chapter One

# 'In Utter Poverty'

### *The First Letter to Agnes of Prague*[1] *Before June 11, 1234*

[1]To the esteemed and most holy virgin, Lady Agnes, daughter of the most excellent and illustrious king of Bohemia, [2]Clare, unworthy servant of Jesus Christ and *useless* servant (cf. Luke 17:10) of the enclosed Ladies of the monastery of San Damiano, her subject and servant in all things, presents herself totally with a special reverence that she attain the glory of everlasting happiness (cf. Sirach 50:5).

[3]As I hear of the fame of Your holy conduct and irreproachable life, which is known not only to me but to the entire world as well, *I* greatly rejoice and exult in the Lord (Habakkuk 3:18). [4]I am not alone in rejoicing at such great news, but [I am joined by] all who serve and seek to serve Jesus Christ. [5]For, though You, more than others, could have enjoyed the magnificence and honor and dignity of the world and could have been married to the illustrious emperor with splendor befitting You and His Excellency, [6]You have rejected all these things and have chosen with Your whole heart and soul a life of holy poverty and destitution. [7]Thus You took a spouse of a more noble lineage, Who will keep Your virginity ever unspotted and unsullied, the Lord Jesus Christ.

[8]"When You have loved [Him], You are chaste;
when you have touched [Him], You become more pure;
when you have accepted [Him], You are a virgin.

[9]Whose power is stronger,
Whose generosity more abundant,
Whose appearance more beautiful,
Whose love more tender,
Whose courtesy more gracious.

[10]In Whose embrace You are already caught up;
Who has adorned Your breast with precious stones
and has placed priceless pearls on Your ears
[11]and has surrounded You with sparkling gems
as though blossoms of springtime
and placed on Your head *a golden crown*
*as a sign of Your holiness.*

[12]Therefore, most beloved sister, or should I say, Lady, worthy of great respect: because You are the spouse and the mother and the sister of my Lord Jesus Christ (cf. 2 Corinthians 11:2; Matthew 12:50), [13]and have been beautifully adorned with the sign of an undefiled virginity and a most holy poverty: Be strengthened in the holy service which You have undertaken out of a burning desire for the poor Crucified, [14]Who for the sake of all of us took upon Himself the Passion of the Cross (Hebrews 12:2), delivered us from the power of the Prince of Darkness (Colossians 1:13) to whom we were enslaved because of the disobedience of our first parent, and so reconciled us to God the Father (2 Corinthians 5:18).

[15]O blessed poverty,
who bestows eternal riches
on those who love and embrace her!
[16]O holy poverty,
God promises the kingdom of heaven
and, in fact, offers eternal glory and a blessed life
to those who possess and desire you!

[17]O God-centered poverty,
whom the Lord Jesus Christ
Who ruled and now rules heaven and earth,
Who spoke and things were made,
condescended to embrace before all else!

[18]The foxes have dens, He says, and the birds of the air have nests, but the Son of Man, Christ, has nowhere to lay His head (Matthew 8:20), but bowing His head gave up His spirit (John 19:30).

[19]If so great and good a Lord, then, on coming into the Virgin's womb, chose to appear despised, needy, and poor in this world [20]so that people who were in utter poverty, want and absolute need of heavenly nourishment might become rich in Him by possessing the kingdom of heaven, [21]*be* very joyful and glad (cf. Habbabuk 3:18)! Be filled with a remarkable happiness and a spiritual joy! [22]because, since contempt of the world has pleased You more than its honors, poverty more than earthly riches, and You have sought to store up greater treasures in heaven rather than on earth, [23]*where* rust does not consume nor moth destroy nor thieves break in and *steal* (cf. Matthew 6:20), Your reward is very rich in heaven! [24]And You have truly merited to be called sister, spouse and mother (cf. 2 Corinthians 11:2; Matthew 12:50) of the Son of the Most High Father and of the glorious Virgin.

[25]You know, I believe, that the kingdom of heaven is promised and given by the Lord only to the poor (cf. Matthew 5:3) for she who loves temporal things loses the fruit of love. [26]Such a person *cannot serve God and money,* for either the one is loved and the other hated, or the one is served and the other despised (cf. Matthew 6:24).

[27]You also know that one who is clothed cannot fight another who is naked, because she is more quickly thrown who gives her adversary a chance to get hold of her; [28]and that one who lives in the glory of earth cannot rule with Christ in heaven.

Again [You know] that it is easier for a camel to pass through the eye of a needle than for a rich person to enter the kingdom of heaven (Matthew 19:24). [29]Therefore, You have cast aside Your garments, that is, earthly riches, that You might not be overcome by the one fighting against You [and] You might enter the kingdom of heaven through the straight path and the narrow gate (cf. Matthew 7:13-14).

[30]What a great and praiseworthy exchange:
to leave the things of time for those of eternity,
to choose the things of heaven for the goods of earth,
to receive the hundred-fold in place of one,
and *to possess* a blessed eternal *life*.

[31]Because of this I have resolved, as best I can, to beg Your Excellency and Your holiness by humble prayers in the mercy of Christ, to be strengthened in His holy service, [32]and to progress from good to better, from virtue to virtue (cf. Psalms 83:8), that He Whom You serve with the total desire of Your soul may bestow on You the reward for which You so long.

[33]I also beg You in the Lord, as much as I can, to include in Your holy prayers (cf. Romans 15:30) me, Your servant, though useless (cf. Luke 17:10), and the other sisters with me in the monastery, who are all devoted to You, [34]that by their help we may merit the mercy of Jesus Christ, and together with You may merit to enjoy the everlasting vision.

[35]Farewell in the Lord. And pray for me (cf. 1 Thessalonians 5:25).

## *The Mystery of Human Beings*

In what way are human beings so poor? We are in "absolute need of heavenly nourishment" (1 LAg 20), Clare writes to Agnes. On our own, without God, we do not have what could satiate our hunger, could fulfill this "absolute need." Whether or not we are aware of it, we hunger for absolute happiness. This is not a small issue. It is a fundamental question: how are we to manage the poverty and the indigence that are imposed on us by the human condition? How are we to resolve the question of the deepest desire dwelling in us?

Whether we are conscious of it or not, throughout our lives we are seeking to fill the abyss of this fundamental desire. We can keep the yearning at a distance. We can judge it, choose it, endure it, reject it, question it or accept it. Herein lies our uniqueness in the midst of creation. Now, how are we to judge this desire? Where are we poor and needy human beings going in the heart of the universe? While we sense the possibility of infinite greatness in the midst of our poverty, where are we going? According to Clare, this infinite of which we have some sense is not an evanescent greatness. It will not evaporate or disappear. Our essential deprivation and our fundamental need to possess the fullness of life in the blossoming of our being are at the root of all human desires. Clare considers the presence of this yearning as a positive value. However, because this yearning is essential and ineradicable, it can offer an opportunity for us or a perilous risk.

Human existence appears as a path where, from birth to death, we stumble against the unknown. When we look back, our birth is accomplished and it does not belong to us: we were brought to life. When we look ahead, we stumble against the wall of our unthinkable disappearance. Death is ineluctable, and yet we cannot conceive of it as our death. This lack of knowledge from the start to the end of our lives produces pressing questions in us: Who am I? What is my origin? Where am I going? This implacable aspect of life, linked with becoming conscious of our becoming, projects us forward in a search for meaning. There is in us a certain dynamism inviting us to go beyond the limits of the human condition.

Have we meditated enough on the distress of humans crushed by the weight of the realities of their own lives: their weaknesses, their limitations, their sufferings and their deaths? The distress at stake here is not mere ignorance. It is something incurable and something very subtle to formulate.

Whatever the system of government and society may be, each day we find ourselves faced with the dullness of daily routine. We live in the familiar circle of what we do with our hands, see with our eyes and what we feel in our hearts. We can know all that is said about international events. We can have a great culture and know all that has been written on the history of past centuries and even millennia. Yet, no certainty of meaning for us emerges from all that. Moreover, we live with the mystery that we are to ourselves and we live in perpetual amazement about life and its triviality.

Why go on with this description? Each one of us can recognize himself or herself in it. What is important in the end? Is it not to let the unfathomable depth of our being come to truth with an open heart? Because we are fully caught up in what we are doing, we often do not know our lives very well. We have to live, at our own risk, the quest for a meaning that cannot move faster than we do and cannot tell us anything yet. We are not going over a preplanned blueprint of our lives. Instead we are charting something new.

### *The Secret Expectations of Human Beings*

In very simple words, words with deep implications, Clare is telling us fundamentally poor and needy human beings, that we are harboring secret expectations within ourselves. These countless and far-reaching expectations are, at times, consoling and, at other times, they are distressing to us.

There is no shame or absurdity in desiring: this is undoubtedly the first and fundamental principle that Clare suggests. We will not understand what Clare means if we do not see ourselves as hungry beings and if we refuse to accept the hunger and thirst that torment us. Let us not think that by putting her finger on our fundamental yearning, Clare sought only to disclose the extent to which we are incomplete and empty. Did not we already know it? What is important for Clare is to guide our eyes to human beings in search of truth.

Before the grandiose manifestations of natural forces, before the immensity of unsatisfied desires dwelling in us, before the mysteries of life and death, we have come to understand that the universe escaped our control. This is the reason why, throughout time and space, we have always clung to truths that are more or less demonstrable. At present, this is a vast market that is constantly fed by imports from the West and, above all, from the East: traditional religions or different forms of new religiosity. All these beliefs represent our attempts to understand the divine, the human condition and what is awaiting us after death. However, all of that should not be placed on the same level.

Where do human beings get the idea that there could be a God or, rather, "something divine"? Thinkers of all times and cultures must have taken this aspect of the human spirit into consideration. Thus, one part of philosophy is called "metaphysics," that is, the study of what is beyond the *phusis*,[2] or "nature." As a matter of fact, nature appears as the visible aspect of a mystery whose essential part is invisible. In the thirteenth century, Saint Thomas Aquinas spoke of rational ways to reach God. For medieval thinkers, Saint Thomas in particular, their knowledge of God and their relationship with God were solidly rooted in their Christian faith. It was only in a second phase that they sought to show the rationality and the validity of that faith. They wanted to create a bridge between faith, which for them was the response to a revelation, and human reason. In the eighteenth century, there occurred a change of direction in the search. It was the beginning of the era of the cult of nature and reason. There was an attempt to deduce God from these two realities. The source of faith would no longer be God's revelation but instead human reasoning. This was *deism*, a belief in a God postulated by nature and by reason, the administrator of the natural order and of the moral order. In its principle, deism was limited to recognizing the existence of God as a Supreme Being but without a precise, personal bond with creatures and without revelation or dogma.[3] Deism marks an important step toward atheism, in the sense that it produces a particular image of God: God in the image of natural processes, God as the "great architect of the world," the supreme artisan of creation. Yet, this way of thinking ignores the fact that God cannot be confined in any concept or in any representation that human beings may have of God. By definition, the being of God is far beyond the resources of our vocabulary.

### *Christ, the Way, the Truth and the Life of Human Beings*

To encounter God in Clare's writings is to discover that God is always escaping us and that the limits of such an encounter are not in God but, rather, in us. Our request to see, understand or to grasp God is subject to the representation we have of God. God's horizon is much vaster than all our representations. This horizon is so sweeping that we cannot circumscribe it nor enclose it in our ways of conceiving it.

God is fully God, radically other and different from us, more present to us than we are present to God. "Where is your God?" (Psalm 42:3). This question that, in different ways, life is constantly asking of us, is found at the heart of Clare's religious experience. In her thought and writing, the first thing we grasp about God is the longing stirred up in us by God, a longing that is never satisfied through the idols we unceasingly propose to it.

We have to let God be God while we move forward in our understanding of what God is without ever fully grasping, enclosing or mastering God in a game of pre-established questions and answers. The understanding we may have of God's mystery cannot have access to the full divine light without the very revelation of God himself. God alone can reveal the divine.

Clare's thought lies squarely within the truth of Christian faith. This faith is based on the revelation that God gave us of his own mystery and of his plan of salvation for us by sending to us his Son, Jesus Christ, the Son who is God's Word as it is expressed in the letter to the Hebrews: "Long ago God spoke to our ancestors in many and various ways by the prophets, but in these last days he has spoken to us by a Son, whom he appointed heir of all things, through whom he also created the worlds" (Hebrews 1:1–2).

After the Son no new messengers are sent. God's revelation of God in the Son cannot be surpassed. In Jesus, God has told us everything, and in some ways, God does not have anything else to tell us that could satisfy our curiosity.

For Clare Christ is the truth of human beings. But Clare understood very well that God's revelation in Jesus Christ cannot be confined once and for all within the limits of our representations. This revelation necessarily demands that we pass through the negation of all our assertions about God. Is God all-powerful? With Clare we can say yes, provided that we do not forget that this all-powerfulness is expressed through the all-weakness of this "God Who was placed poor in the crib, lived poor in the world, and remained naked on the cross" (TestCl 45).

Is God supreme beauty? Indeed, Clare asserts, provided we accept that his beauty burst forth on the cross.

"Your Spouse, though more beautiful than the children of men (Psalm 44:3) became, for your salvation, the lowest of men, was despised, struck, scourged untold times throughout His entire body, and then died amid the suffering of the Cross" (2 LAg 20).

In Clare's view, Christian mystical experience achieves an encounter, a knowledge of and an existential communion with Christ. According to Clare, Christ is telling us that we do not have to look very far for what can pacify us. Nothing will ever satisfy us if not what we ourselves have chosen, the food before which we will remain free. Any action that we cannot really claim as our own and that escapes us can only disappoint our infinite desire: we must neither consent to it nor want to return to it. Instead, we have to give it up and reject it. An action is not good merely because it is not ours. It is somehow imposed upon us by a violence that, in the final analysis, can only make us suffer, as Paul says:

> I do not understand my own actions. For I do not do what I want, but I do the very thing I hate. Now if I do what I do not want, I agree that the law is good. But in fact it is no longer I that do it, but sin that dwells within me. For I know that nothing good dwells within me, that is, in my flesh. I can will what is right, but I cannot do it. For I do not do the good I want, but the evil I do not want is what I do. Now if I do what I do not want, it is no longer I that do it, but sin that dwells within me. (Romans 7:15–20)

## *Desire and Temptation*

Human life is filled with tumult and conflict amid all the forms of desire. At the root of all our human desires, we find our essential poverty and our fundamental craving to possess life in the full blossoming of our being. This positive desire is in keeping with the nature that God consecrates. All of Clare's writing confirms this fundamental notion. However, because desire is something essential and ineradicable in us, it can also become a permanent and dangerous temptation for us. Desire can be perverted by "the enemy of the human race" who seeks to destroy us by the glitter of temporary and deceptive glory. Then we need a great deal of strength and courage to resist this enemy. As Clare says in her third letter to Agnes, "Who would not dread the treacheries of the enemy of humanity who, through the arrogance of momentary and deceptive glories, attempts to reduce to nothing that which is greater than heaven itself?" (3 LAg 20).

At the starting point of human life, Clare establishes the connection between the mystery of human poverty and the mystery of sin. We are created to live in harmony with God and with others. Sociability forms part of our very nature. Human plenitude is found in our openness to God and to others. But, in this perspective, sin appears as a rupture of relationships. What does sin consist of? A supreme act of self-centeredness and egotism. This is why Clare insists with her sisters: "I admonish and exhort the sisters in the Lord Jesus Christ to beware of all pride, vainglory, envy, avarice, care and anxiety about this world, detraction and murmuring, dissension and division" (RCl 10, 6).

Instead of turning to God and to other people, we human beings always have a tendency to close in on ourselves. We are tempted to make our own selves into the supreme riches. We forget that at the core of our beings we are created to live in openness to God and to others. In the end, we find ourselves with only meager riches as our treasure: our own self-image in the delusion of wanting to take God's place. We fail to see that our true riches consist precisely in getting outside of ourselves, in our capacity to open up to God and to other people, and we do not see that we would be fulfilled only to the extent we were poor. In fact, it is only freely chosen poverty of the heart that can enrich us. Here we are stumbling against the apparent paradox of our human poverty in light of God's plan: the more our hearts are poor, the more we will find our plenitude and our wealth. The more we seek to be rich in ourselves and full of self-conceit, the poorer we become. This is the sum total of Clare's mysticism as it is expressed in all her writings.

With a great deal of insight, Clare shows how evil (pride) is brought about by a decision of our will that sets us up against good, God, other people and against the meaning of existence by the exaggerated perception that we have of our own personal value. When Clare puts pride at the top of the list of all human evils (RCl 10, 6), she is not denouncing a few petty vanities, but she is referring to our fundamental refusal to acknowledge our limits and, in particular, what we owe to God and others. This is the path of sin in our midst as it breeds disorders and struggles and creates hatred and irremediable hostilities in society. Clare understood how the effectiveness of evil in this world is manifested by all that closes us in on ourselves. In connection with that, Clare speaks of envy (*individia):* ill will, jealousy; avarice *(avaritia):* greed, cupidity; worldly concern and preoccupation (*cura et sollicitudo huius saeculi*): preoccupation with the glitter of temporary glory; criticism (*detractio*): slander, defamation; murmuring (*murmur*): grumbling, interior murmuring; dissension (*dissensio*): dissent, discord and division (*divisio*).

In simple but strong terms, at the risk of offending our sensitivity, Clare mercilessly underscores our corruption, our selfishness and our sin. She evokes the weakness that is hidden at the core of our desires. The flesh and the heart are clamoring at the same time and, sometimes, we believe this clamor arises from the same desire: "our flesh is not bronze nor is our strength that of stone (Job 6:12). No, we are frail and inclined to every bodily weakness" (3 LAg 38–39).

This weakness, this flaw that is already deep within us, makes us capable of sinking deeper into sin at any time.

Then our frailty is only a figure of our injured strength that has to be healed. Clare insists on the fact that human beings can lust after foods that do not help them to live:

> You know, I believe, that the kingdom of heaven is promised and given by the Lord only to the poor... for she who loves temporal things loses the fruit of love. Such a person *cannot serve God and money*, for either the one is loved and the other hated, or the one is served and the other despised. . . . You also know that one who is clothed cannot fight another who is naked, because she is more quickly thrown who gives her adversary a chance to get hold of her; and that one who lives in the glory of earth cannot rule with Christ in heaven. (1 LAg 25-28)

For Clare, death is a result of our disorderly appetites. They destroy us because when desire feeds upon itself, as if we could give it real food, it reduces us to nothing at all. Clare discloses, in full light, the recesses and tricks of selfishness. Its egocentric movement, bent on hoarding material and social space, responding to processes that we do not always perceive and which, when all is said and done, destroy us. "How many kings and queens of this world let themselves be deceived, for, even though their pride may reach the skies and their heads touch the clouds, in the end they are as forgotten as a dung-heap" (3 LAg 27–28).

### *The Limitation and the Greatness of Human Beings*

"Man is the only creature who refuses to be what he is," Albert Camus wrote in his book *The Rebel*.[4] When we consider our limitations, our weakness and our sin, we are always dreaming of being something other than what we are. However, at one time or another in our lives, we find ourselves forced to make a choice. Either we rebel, we refuse the limited creature that life forces us to be and this attitude dooms us to despair and to death or, without renouncing the realities of our human condition, we learn to accept our limitations, to marvel at the greatness of life and at all that is positive in existence. The latter is the attitude that heals us from ourselves. It hurls us into a kind of light that fulfills us at the same time as it frees us from ourselves because, in this attitude, we lose sight of ourselves. Our primary human task consists, therefore, in constantly taking up the act by which we welcome the gift of existence. An act of receptivity which, in the same movement, allows the power of communicating life to arise in us. We turn to the One from whom this gift comes in order to remain in this presence without seeking to restrict or reduce anything. Believers will say: God precedes us. Ahead of us, there is that Being whom we call God, through whom and in whom all that is has its existence.

Clare introduces us to this attitude of faith in what we are—men and women created in the image of God. She invites us to journey in life with others and with ourselves and to build up confidence.[5] According to Clare, all that is good, beautiful, true, just and powerful in human beings finds its culmination in Christ. Thus, in June 1234, in a letter addressed to Agnes of Prague, Clare presents Christ with the human and specifically masculine qualities of Frederick II, Agnes's former suitor:

> As I hear of the fame of Your holy conduct and irreproachable life, which is known not only to me but to the entire world as well, *I* greatly rejoice and exult in the Lord . . . I am not alone in rejoicing at such great news, but [I am joined by] all who serve and seek to serve Jesus Christ. For, though You, more than others, could have enjoyed the magnificence and honor and dignity of the world and could have been married to the illustrious emperor with splendor befitting You and His Excellency, You have rejected all these things and have chosen with Your whole heart and soul a life of holy poverty and destitution. Thus You took a spouse of a more noble lineage, Who will

keep Your virginity ever unspotted and unsullied,
the Lord Jesus Christ.

"When You have loved [Him], You are chaste;
when you have touched [Him], You become
more pure;
when you have accepted [Him], You are a virgin.

Whose power is stronger,
Whose generosity more abundant,
Whose appearance more beautiful,
Whose love more tender,
Whose courtesy more gracious.

In Whose embrace You are already caught up;
Who has adorned Your breast with precious stones
and has placed priceless pearls on Your ears
and has surrounded You with sparkling gems
as though blossoms of springtime
and placed on Your head a *golden crown*
*as a sign of Your holiness.*" (1 LAg 3-11)

Here, Clare employs seemingly romantic language to praise Christ as the noblest, the strongest and the most handsome of men. What is the meaning of this reality for believers? It means that, in themselves, men and women have divine qualities of nobility, strength, generosity and beauty. It also means that the one whose love is the most extraordinary because it surpasses everything is the only one who can completely fulfill human beings. The human love that is possible between a man and a woman is in the image of God's love in which human love finds its absolute plenitude. This love is God and God's mystery, infinitely surpassing all that pertains to our human experience, whether in conjugal love, friendship, beauty or generosity. These human values are signs of God's love instilled in humankind. However, God is the only fullness that can give men and women stability in the love that is experienced in this world. This is what Clare's deeply theological language suggests.

The contemplation of the mystery of truth and of divine poverty inspires Clare to look for what can lead us to God in the beauty and greatness of human life. With great insight Clare evokes the realism of human life, which she enhances in light of the humanity of the Son of God.

Within these reflections, the gospel is beginning to speak of what makes us human among humans. Clare's writings are evangelical, in the sense that, like the gospel, they touch upon something immutable in us: our frail human nature is loved by God and called to life. Expressed another way, these texts are essentially spiritual writings that reveal to us our own face in the face of Christ.

## *Notes*

[1] "This first letter was written before Pentecost [June 11] 1234, that is to say, before Agnes joined the [Prague] monastery: Clare only calls her 'daughter of the King of Bohemia' and addresses her with the formal 'vous'" (Jean-François Godet, in Claire d'Assise, *Ecrits* [Paris: Editions du Cerf, Coll. "Sources chrétiennes," no. 325, 1985], p. 18).

[2] This Greek word evokes the idea of inflation, of sprouting, in the sense of ideas that appeared later under the term of "nature" (from the Latin *natura*, from *nasci*, "to be born," a translation of the Greek *phusis*).

[3] Biblical religion is based on historical revelation. The latter does not depend on the teaching of a single founder. In fact, we see it develop during fifteen or twenty centuries before it reached its fullness in Christ, the revealer, par excellence. For Christians, believing means welcoming this Revelation which has come to them through humankind. Dogmas are papal or conciliar propositions that the church teaches as being revealed by God, so that negating them constitutes a heresy.

[4] "Man is the only creature who refuses to be what he is. The question is to know if this refusal can only lead him to destroy others and himself, if every revolt has to end up in the justification of universal murder or if, on the contrary, without claiming an impossible innocence, it can discover the principle of a reasonable culpability" (Albert Camus, *The Rebel: An Essay on Man in Revolt*, Anthony Bower, trans. [New York: Vintage Books, 1991], p. 22).

[5] We should focus on the etymology of the word *confidence*: "to have faith in, to trust."

Chapter Two

# That We 'Might Become Rich'

## *The Second Letter to Agnes of Prague*[1] *Between 1234 and 1238*

[1]To the daughter *of the King of kings*, the servant *of the Lord of lords* (Revelation 19:16), the most worthy Spouse of Jesus Christ, and, therefore, the most noble Queen, Lady Agnes: [2]Clare, *the useless* (Luke 17:10) and unworthy servant of the Poor Ladies: greeting and a life always of the highest poverty.

[3]I give thanks to the Giver of grace *from Whom*, we believe, *every good and perfect gift proceeds* (James 1:17), because He has adorned you with such splendors of virtue and illuminated you with such marks of perfection, [4]that, since you have become such a diligent imitator *of the Father of all perfection* (Matthew 5:48), you might be made perfect and His eyes do not see anything imperfect in you.

[5]This is that perfection with which the King himself will take you to Himself in the heavenly bridal chamber where He is seated in glory on a starry throne, [6]because you have despised the splendor of an earthly kingdom and considered of little value the offers of an imperial marriage. [7]Instead, as someone zealous for the holiest poverty, in a spirit of great humility and the most ardent charity, you have held fast *to the footprints* (1 Peter 2:22) of Him to Whom you have merited to be joined as a Spouse.

[8]But since I know that you are adorned with many virtues, I will spare my words and not weary you with endless speech, [9]even though nothing seems superfluous to you if you can draw some consolation from it. [10]But because *one thing is necessary* (Luke 10:42), I bear witness to that one thing and encourage you, for love of Him to Whom you have offered yourself as *a holy* and pleasing *sacrifice* (Romans 12:1), [11]that you always be mindful of your resolution like another Rachel always seeing your beginning (cf. Genesis 29:16).

What you hold, may you [always] hold,
What you do, may you [always] do and never abandon.
[12]But with swift pace, light step,
  unswerving feet,
  so that even your steps stir up no dust,
[13]may you go forward
  securely, joyfully, and swiftly,
  on the path of prudent happiness,
[14]not believing anything,
  not agreeing with anything
   that would dissuade you from this resolution
   or that would place a stumbling block for you on
    the way,
  so that you may offer your vows to the Most High
   in the pursuit of that perfection
      to which the Spirit of the Lord has called you.

[15]In all of this, follow the counsel of our venerable father, our Brother Elias, the Minister General, that you may walk more securely in the way of the commands of the Lord (Psalms 118:32). [16]Prize it beyond the advice of the others and cherish it as dearer to you than any gift. [17]If anyone would tell you something else or suggest something that would hinder your perfection or seem contrary to your divine vocation, even though you must respect him, do not follow his counsel.

[18]But as a poor virgin,
embrace the poor Christ.
[19]Look upon Him Who became contemptible for you,
and follow Him, making yourself contemptible in this world for Him.

[20]Your spouse, though *more beautiful than the children of men* (Psalms 44:3), became, for your salvation, the lowest of men, was despised, struck, scourged untold times throughout His entire body, and then died amid the suffering of the Cross.

O most noble Queen,
gaze upon [Him],
consider [Him]
contemplate [Him].
as you desire to imitate [Him].
[21]If you suffer with Him, *you will reign with Him.*
[If you] weep [with Him], you shall rejoice with Him;
[If you] die with Him on the cross of tribulation,
you shall possess heavenly mansions *in the splendor of the saints*
[22]and, *in the Book of Life*, your *name* shall be called glorious among men.

[23]Because of this you shall share always and forever the glory of the kingdom of heaven in place of earthly and passing things, and everlasting treasures instead of those that perish, and you shall live forever.

[24]Farewell, most dear Sister, yes, and Lady, because of the Lord, your Spouse. [25]Commend me and my sisters in your fervent prayers, for we rejoice in the good things of the Lord that He works in you through His grace. [26]Commend us truly to your sisters as well.

## *The Marvelous Exchange*[2]

Clare is aware that a marvelous exchange[3] has taken place between God and humankind. This is the heart of Christianity she attests to and celebrates in her writings: Christ is the Good News of what God has accomplished for us and for our salvation in his Passover. This salvation event, which concerns not only human beings but the entire universe, manifests that God loved the world and became reconciled with it through Christ's death and resurrection. In the 1234 letter addressed to Agnes, Clare mentions this Good News of the gospel in the following terms:

> Be strengthened in the holy service which You have undertaken out of a burning desire for the poor Crucified, Who for the sake of all of us took upon Himself the Passion of the Cross . . . delivered us from the power of the Prince of Darkness . . . to whom we were enslaved because of the disobedience of our first parent, and so reconciled us to God the Father. . . .
>
> If so great and good a Lord, then, on coming into the Virgin's womb, chose to appear despised, needy, and poor in this world so that people who were in utter poverty, want and absolute need of heavenly nourishment might become rich in Him by possessing the kingdom of heaven, *be* very joyful and glad. . . ! Be filled with a remarkable happiness and a spiritual joy! . . . (1 LAg 13, 14, 19, 20, 21)

Through the revelation in the gospel, God connects with us and deepens our experience. Until then, poor and needy humankind is lost, and we cannot fully conceive of the reasons for this perdition. The doctrine of original sin[4] seems absurd and shocking to many people. Frightening us and filling us with horror, it uncovers the depth of our human history beyond all reasonable, social, psychoanalytic, economic and political developments. Yes, our humanity is lost in original sin.[5] Acknowledging this is neither pessimism nor an act of despair. Clare is convinced that our poverty and our indigence are the only things we can claim as our own. After a long or short human and Christian experience, each and every one of us can come to the same conviction: we are Adam's children, incomplete creatures, blind and inclined to prefer the temporary honors of this world to the glory of God.

When Clare states in her letters that we are members of a lost humanity, she does not intend by that to erase our most original reality, that is, that we are created in God's image and likeness, capable of doing good. Whatever the havoc caused by sin, we are "the most worthy of all creatures" (3 LAg 21) for "the Son of Man came to seek out and to save the lost" (Luke 19:10). "Be strengthened in the holy service which You have undertaken out of a burning desire for the poor Crucified, Who for the sake of all of us took upon Himself the Passion of the Cross . . . delivered us from the power of the Prince of Darkness . . . to whom we were enslaved because of the disobedience of our first parent, and so reconciled us to God the Father" (1 LAg 13–14).

The deep and subtle roots of original sin in us prevent us from welcoming the wonder of our being created in God's image and recreated in Christ's death and resurrection. The marvelous exchange between God and human beings took place once for all at the birth, life and death of Christ. It is, above all, when we meditate on Jesus' passion and death that we can give ourselves to that marvelous exchange because nothing else can justify us and make us holy. Yves Tourenne captured well Clare's spiritual thought:

> The marvelous exchange was already accomplished as far back as the Annunciation and Bethlehem. However, it seems to me that we can really give ourselves to that marvelous exchange only in Jesus' Passion and death because we are lost sinners. Because nothing can justify us and make us holy: nothing, not the Law of Israel, not morality and not

the observances of our religious lives. All that only underscores our inability to love, our pride of Poor Clares and Franciscans, our sins as human beings and as Christians. What can justify us in the strong sense of the term, in the way Martin Luther understood this verb, in the sense where justice in the Bible means participation, in God's name, in God's holiness? It can only happen in faith in the marvelous exchange where God says to us: "Look at my Son. He was made into sin and a curse so that in him, you might become justified and blessed." Christianity has to go this far if it is not to fall back into a morality, or a religion, or a wisdom without salt, if it is to penetrate into the violence of this world in order to "evangelize it." Christianity has to tell the world that we are all evil to the point of killing God, to the point of rendering God powerless in this world but that it is precisely when we have committed the irreversible that Christ, crowned with thorns and pierced, comes to justify us. Our sin has to be disclosed for the marvelous exchange to take place. When I look upon Jesus in his Passion and his death, I discover my own violence but I see even more that, in Christ, God came to take away my violence to give me God's own sweetness, to take away my pride to give me divine respect, to take away my scoffing to give me what I have shown so poorly to others: the compassion, patience and the modesty that lift up the humiliated. There is so much more that should be said about the marvelous exchange which is the salt, the absolute originality of Christianity, the Christianity of the Annunciation, Golgotha, of the Church born of Pentecost, the Christianity which is the only hope that the world can receive if some day sin hurls the earth into ruin, in any case, the only hope that speaks of God by speaking about humans, a hope that glorifies God by admiring humans. This is the most realistic hope there is because it does not conceal our human limitations and our sin.[6]

### *God at the Heart of Human Poverty*

The supreme mystery of Jesus' poverty (poverty of heart and physical poverty) is achieved in his passion and his death. The Lord Jesus Christ does not cast aside his divine nature. However, in order to be "born in human likeness" and to be "found in human form" (Philippians 2:7), he renounces all the radiance of his divine glory in his humanity. As the author of the letter to the Hebrews writes, Christ became "like his brothers and sisters in every respect" (Hebrews 2:17). And, in his letter to the Romans, Paul will specify "in the likeness of sinful flesh" (Romans 8:3), even though Jesus himself did not sin (2 Corinthians 5:21; Hebrews 4:15).

He, the Son, the bearer of God's plenitude, does not become incarnate in perfect humanity (that would already be an unprecedented abasement on his part) but, instead, in sinful humanity doomed to death (cf. 2 Corinthians 5:21). As Clare puts it, he made himself "to appear despised, needy, and poor," with the radical poverty that characterizes the human condition. Although he was God, Jesus Christ became man and shared the condition of sinful humanity, except for one thing: he himself did not sin. Christ becomes man, in a situation of poverty and radical need, because in his eternal mystery, he is total poverty of self. This mystery of God's poverty, at the heart of the Trinity, is refracted, as it were, at the human level. Incarnated, the Son lives the mystery of being Savior of humankind in an event that represents the ultimate point of human poverty: his death on the cross. There, in his passion and his death, he is in the most concrete way, a poor man, one of the men whose body is crushed and whose heart is torn by the sin of humankind. In Jesus, the poverty of God does not only consist in assuming our lost humanity by renouncing the radiance of his glory. In addition, in becoming human, Jesus joins us at the ultimate point of human poverty, in the existential act where poverty encompasses the entire being and every being, to the extent that it is no more than a heap of sufferings. Christ's destiny is the most absolute poverty: he lost everything, including the faith of his people. Scorned by his own, he is dreadfully struck, scourged, drained in his body and his friendships. He dies in the anguish of the cross after crying out from the depth of his being: "My God, my God, why have you forsaken me?" (Matthew 27:46). Here we touch the very depths of human poverty. "All you who pass by the way, / look and see if there is any suffering / like my suffering! / Let us respond / with one voice, / with one spirit, / to Him crying and grieving Who said: / "Remembering this over and over / leaves my soul downcast within me!" (4 LAg 25-26).

### *Salvation and Mystery of Poverty*

Christ takes the consequence of sin to the bitter end with the most extreme realism. However, his physical poverty is illumined from within by the poverty of his heart. Salvation springs from the conjunction of the two sorts of poverty, and from this union also comes the Resurrection that saves and enriches now redeemed humankind with all the glory of God. The Resurrection is not merely a new stage following the cross. The Resurrection is the fruit of the cross. Because of the poverty of his heart, Christ, who became poor to the point of death on the cross, bears many fruits. The lordship of Jesus emerges from his poverty. Our salvation, which is linked to this lordship, comes from Christ's abasement: Christ the Lord comes from the poor Christ. Such is the utter madness of divine Love that the limit of sin, assumed in the poverty of heart of Jesus Christ, becomes salvation and riches for us:

> If so great and good a Lord, then, on coming into the Virgin's womb, chose to appear despised, needy, and poor in this world so that people who were in

> utter poverty, want and absolute need of heavenly nourishment might become rich in Him by possessing the kingdom of heaven. (1LAg 19–20)

The mystery of poverty essentially is part of the mystery of salvation and the gospel. Poverty is evangelical in the strongest sense of the term. It is in and by it that we live the heart of the Good News. Christ's Resurrection is the revelation of the staggering fruitfulness of poverty. Christ the Lord is indeed the "poor Christ" of Nazareth, raised in glory because he lived poverty to the extreme limit of love. All human beings benefit from this rising, not just the oppressed and the hungry but also the richest among us.

We understand that, in her stage of peregrination and wanting to follow "the footprints of the poor and humble Jesus Christ" (3 LAg 4), Clare confers an essential importance to the presence of the mystery of poverty within her. She discovers her own radical misery, the misery of sin, and she strives to be freed from it by deepening in her heart her openness to God and to others. For Clare, following in the footprints of Christ means entering into Christ's attitude. She writes to Agnes:

> But as a poor virgin,
> embrace the poor Christ.
> Look upon Him Who became contemptible for you,
> and follow Him, making yourself contemptible in this world for Him.
>
> Your spouse, though *more beautiful than the children of men*... became, for your salvation, the lowest of men, was despised, struck, scourged untold times throughout His entire body, and then died amid the suffering of the Cross.
>
> O most noble Queen,
> gaze upon [Him],
> consider [Him]
> contemplate [Him].
> as you desire to imitate [Him].

> If you suffer with Him, *you will reign with Him.*
> [If you] weep [with Him], you shall rejoice with Him;
> [If you] die with Him on the cross of tribulation,
> you shall possess heavenly mansions *in the splendor of the saints*
> and, *in the Book of Life*, your *name* shall be called glorious among men.
>
> Because of this you shall share always and forever the glory of the kingdom of heaven in place of earthly and passing things, and everlasting treasures instead of those that perish, and you shall live forever. (2 LAg 18-23)

Poverty is at the very heart of Clare's spiritual thought. It conditions her evangelical mission, and in her it is the continuation of Christ's abasement. Because the church is the body of Christ and the world's salvation has to be continued in and through the church, Clare becomes aware that the poverty manifested in the mystery of Jesus has to be permanently continued in her community in the heart of the church:

> For this reason, on bended knees...I commend all my sisters, both those present and those to come, the holy Mother, the Roman Church, the supreme Pontiff, and, especially, the Lord Cardinal who has been appointed for the Order of Friars Minor and for us, that out of love of the God Who was placed poor in a crib, lived poor in the world, and remained naked on the cross, [our Protector] may always see to it that his little flock...which the Lord Father has begotten in His holy Church by the word and example of our blessed father Francis by following the poverty and humility of His beloved Son and His glorious Virgin Mother, observe the holy poverty that we have promised to God and our most blessed father Saint Francis. May he always encourage and support them in these things. (TCl 44–47)

For Clare, poverty inevitably must become an essential characteristic of her community in the heart of the church simply because the latter is in Christ and receives the mission to make the Easter salvation present here on earth. Because of the church's mission of salvation and the responsibility that its Lord entrusted to it for the proclamation and concretization of the gospel, the church must renounce prestige and any form of power and domination if it does not want to be separated from its Lord. This is the choice that the church must make at any cost. This is the path to follow in order to have eternal life: "What you hold, may you [always] hold, / What you do, may you [always] do and never abandon. / But with swift pace, light step, / unswerving feet, / so that even your steps stir up no dust, / may you go forward / securely, joyfully, and swiftly, / on the path of prudent happiness, / not believing anything, / not agreeing with anything / that would dissuade you from this resolution / or that would place a stumbling block for you on the way. . ." (2 LAg 11–14).

Thus, by her spiritual intuition, Clare has captured this hidden aspect of the mystery of the living God, which the apostle Paul reveals to us in these terms: "For you know the generous act of our Lord Jesus Christ, that though he was rich, yet for your sakes he became poor, so that by his poverty you might become rich" (2 Corinthians 8:9).

Here we are in the presence of an insurmountable paradox if we attempt to understand it employing reason only: In the Son, God makes us rich by his own poverty! Clare often refers to this text from Scripture (2 Corinthians 8:9). Starting with this intuition, Clare reflects on the human condition.

## *Notes*

[1] This "second letter was written between 1234 and 1238, during the generalate of Elias of Assisi (1232-1239)" (Jean-François Godet, in Claire d'Assise, *Ecrits* [Paris: Editions du Cerf, Coll. "Sources chrétiennes," no. 325, 1985], p. 18).

[2] The "great and praiseworthy exchange" (1 LAg 30) is one of many borrowings of Clare (like Francis of Assisi) from the liturgy. It is the start of the first of the five antiphons of the Feast of the Circumcision (first and second evening prayers).

[3] "The theme of commerce, exchange is one of the privileged themes of early Franciscan thought on poverty: cf. *Sacrum Commercium S. Francisci cum Domina Paupertate,* Quarracchi, 1929" (ECl, p. 91, note). First the exchange designates the commerce of material goods, merchandise itself, the contract which binds the parties on that occasion. In a broader sense, we speak of an exchange of spiritual goods. This is the meaning of the term in Clare's thought: "What a great and praiseworthy exchange: / to leave the things of time for those of eternity, / to choose the things of heaven for the goods of earth, / to receive the hundred-fold in place of one, / and *to possess* a blessed eternal *life*!" (1 LAg 30).

[4] Original sin is the state in which all of us are born. The cause of this sinful condition is the first, or original, sin, the sin of Adam, as the first man and the ancestor of humankind (Genesis 3). Because of that sin, all human beings are, before God, in a situation of being deprived of salvation, something that affects us in the depths of our being. In spite of that, such a sin must not be confused with personal sin freely committed.

[5] The true nature of original sin, its insidiousness, its dimensions may be found in Scripture. There we learn that this revelation about humans is also a revelation about God, about God's love that is opposed by sin and about God's mercy. Indeed, salvation history is the history of the repeated, untiring attempts by God the Creator to snatch us away from sin. In Genesis, God is looking for the man lost by sin and says to him: "Where are you?" (Genesis 3:9).

[6] Yves Tourenne, O.F.M., "L'Admirable Echange," ch. 1, no. 2, "L'Admirable Echange, un échange crucifiant," pp. 7–8.

## Chapter Three

# 'The Most Worthy of All Creatures'

### *The Third Letter to Agnes of Prague*[1] *Early 1238*

[1]To the lady [who is] most respected in Christ and the sister loved more than all [other] human beings, Agnes, sister of the illustrious king of Bohemia, but now *the sister and spouse* of the Most High King of heaven (cf. Matthew 12:50; 2 Corinthians 11:2); [2]Clare, the most lowly and unworthy handmaid of Christ and servant of the Poor Ladies: the joys of redemption *in the Author of Salvation* (Hebrews 2:10) and every good thing that can be desired.

[3]I am filled with such joys at your well-being, happiness, and marvelous progress through which, I understand, you have advanced in the path you have undertaken to win *a* heavenly *prize* (cf. Philippians 3:14). [4]And I sigh with so much more exultation in the Lord as I have known and believe that you supply more wonderfully what is lacking both in me and in the other sisters in following the footprints of the poor and humble Jesus Christ.

[5]Truly I can rejoice and no one can rob me of such joy [6]since, having at last what under heaven I have desired, I see that, helped by a special gift of wisdom from the mouth of God Himself and in an awe-inspiring and unexpected way, you have brought to ruin the subtleties of our crafty enemy, the pride that destroys human nature, and the vanity that infatuates human hearts. [7][I see, too] that by humility, the virtue of faith, and the strong arms of

poverty, you have taken hold of that *incomparable treasure hidden in the field* of the world and of the human heart (cf. Matthew 13:44), with which you have purchased that by Whom all things have been made from nothing. [8]And, to use the words of the Apostle himself in their proper sense, I consider you *a co-worker of God* Himself (cf. 1 Corinthians 3:9; Romans 16:3) and a support of the weak members of His ineffable Body.

[9]Who is there, then, who would not encourage me to rejoice over such marvelous joys? [10]Therefore, dearly beloved, may you too *always rejoice in the Lord* (Philippians 4:4). [11]And may neither bitterness nor a cloud [of sadness] overwhelm you, O dearly beloved Lady in Christ, joy of the angels and crown of your sisters!

[12]Place your mind before the mirror of eternity!
Place your soul *in the brilliance of glory*!
[13]Place your heart *in the figure of the* divine *substance*!
And *transform* your entire being *into the image*
of the Godhead Itself through contemplation.

[14]So that you too may feel what His friends feel
as they taste *the hidden sweetness*
that God Himself has reserved from the beginning
for those who love Him.

[15]And, after all who ensnare their blind lovers
in a deceitful and turbulent world
have been completely sent away,
you may totally love Him
Who gave Himself totally for your love,
[16]Whose beauty the sun and the moon admire,
Whose rewards and their preciousness and greatness
are without end;
[17]I am speaking of Him
Who is the Son of the Most High,
Whom the Virgin brought to birth
and remained a virgin after His birth.

[18]May you cling to His most sweet Mother who gave birth to a Son whom the heavens could not contain, [19]And yet she carried Him in the little enclosure of her holy womb and held Him on her virginal lap.

[20]Who would not dread the treacheries of the enemy of humanity who, through the arrogance of momentary and deceptive glories, attempts to reduce to nothing that which is greater than heaven itself? [21]Indeed, it is now clear that the soul of a faithful person, the most worthy of all creatures because of the grace of God, is greater than heaven itself, [22]since the heavens and the rest of creation cannot contain their Creator and only the faithful soul is His dwelling place and throne, and this only through the charity that the wicked lack. [23][He Who is] the Truth has said: *Whoever loves me will be loved by My Father, and I too shall love him, and We shall come to him and make Our dwelling place with him* (John 14:21, 23).

[24]As the glorious Virgin of virgins carried [Him] materially, [25]so you, too, *by following in her footprints* (cf. 1 Peter 2:21), especially [those] of poverty and humility, can, without any doubt, always carry Him spiritually in your chaste and virginal body, [26]holding Him by Whom you and *all things are held together* (Wisdom 1:7) possessing that which, in comparison with the other transitory possessions of this world you will possess more securely. [27]How many kings and queens of this world let themselves be deceived, [28]for, even though their pride may reach the skies and their heads touch the clouds, in the end they are as forgotten as a dung-heap!

[29]Now concerning those matters that you have asked me to clarify for you: [30]which are the specific feasts our most glorious Father Saint Francis urged us to celebrate in a special way by a change of food—feasts of which, I believe, you already have some knowledge—I propose to respond to your love.

[31]Your prudence should know, then, that except for the weak and the sick, for whom [Saint Francis] advised

and admonished us to show every possible discretion in matters of food, [32]none of us who are healthy and strong should eat anything other than Lenten fare, either on ferial days or on feast days. [33]Thus, we must fast every day except Sundays and the Nativity of the Lord, on which days we may have two meals. [34]And on ordinary Thursdays everyone may do as she wishes, so that she who does not wish to fast is not obliged. [35]However, we who are well should fast every day except on Sundays and on Christmas.

[36]During the entire Easter week, as the writing of Saint Francis tells us, and on the feasts of the Blessed Virgin Mary and of the holy Apostles, we are not obliged to fast, unless these feasts occur on a Friday. [37]And, as I have already said, let we who are well and strong always eat Lenten fare.

[38]But *our flesh is not bronze nor is our strength that of stone* (Job 6:12). [39]No, we are frail and inclined to every bodily weakness! [40]I beg you, therefore, dearly beloved, to refrain wisely and prudently from an indiscreet and impossible austerity in the fasting that you have undertaken. [41]And I beg you in the Lord to praise the Lord by your very life, to offer the Lord your *reasonable service* (Romans 12:1) and your *sacrifice* always *seasoned with salt* (Leviticus 2:13).

[42]May you do well in the Lord, as I hope I myself do. And remember me and my sisters in your prayers.

## *Joy and the Hidden Treasure*

In her 1238 letter, Claire wishes Agnes the "joys of redemption in the Author of Salvation... and every good thing that can be desired" (3 LAg 2). The revelation of the author of salvation (God, creator and savior) produces overflowing joy in her. In the Old Testament, in the history of Israel, joy rested on the men and women of the Scriptures who recognized God's work through the ages. In the New

Testament, the coming of the Savior creates an atmosphere of joy that Luke, more than the other evangelists, made tangible. Even before rejoicing over his birth (Luke 1:14), when Mary visits Elizabeth, John the Baptist leaped for joy in his mother's womb (Luke 1:41–44). With as much joy as humility, the Virgin Mary, whom the angel's greeting had invited to joy (Luke 1:28), sings to the Lord she carries in her womb (Luke 1:42, 46–55). The birth of Jesus brings great joy to the angels announcing it and to the people he is coming to save (Luke 2:10–13; Matthew 1:21). This birth fulfills the expectation of the just who, like Abraham, were already exultant in thinking about it (John 8:56). In Saint Paul, it means the joy of hope, a joy that is connected with trial and suffering. For Paul, joy is one of the fruits of the Spirit (Galatians 5:22). It is not a matter of fleeting enthusiasm but, instead, it is the spiritual joy of believers in the midst of trials (1 Thessalonians 1:6ff.). The perfect joy of Francis of Assisi[2] is a way of living the most difficult situations: even at the heart of the ordeal, there is a kind of deep serenity in which we find salvation. In Clare, we find this permanent, glowing proclamation of joy present everywhere. A path of Christian hope, joy is also marked by trial and solitude:

> Truly I can rejoice and no one can rob me of such joy since, having at last what under heaven I have desired, I see that, helped by a special gift of wisdom from the mouth of God Himself and in an awe-inspiring and unexpected way, you have brought to ruin the subtleties of our crafty enemy, the pride that destroys human nature, and the vanity that infatuates human hearts. [I see, too] that by humility, the virtue of faith, and the strong arms of poverty, you have taken hold of that *incomparable treasure hidden in the field* of the world and of the human heart. . . with which you have purchased that by Whom all things have been made from nothing. And, to use the words of the Apostle himself in their proper sense, I consider you *a co-worker of God* Himself. . . and a support

> of the weak members of His ineffable Body.
>
> Who is there, then, who would not encourage me to rejoice over such marvelous joys? Therefore, dearly beloved, may you too *always rejoice in the Lord.* ... And may neither bitterness nor a cloud [of sadness] overwhelm you, O dearly beloved Lady in Christ, joy of the angels and crown of your sisters! (3 LAg 5–11)

Imagery for the source of Clare's joy is taken from Scripture, especially from the passage from the Gospel on the "hidden treasure": "The kingdom of heaven is like treasure hidden in a field, which someone found and hid; then in his joy he goes and sells all that he has and buys that field" (Matthew 13:44).

Clare uses the image of the "treasure" and gives it a special meaning: it is the yearning for God. What is this desire that is deeply rooted in everyone's heart? Is it not that fundamental need in us to love and to be loved? This is a need to be born anew, to start a new life in the heart of God who awaits us. The kingdom of heaven is precisely this blossoming of life, of light and of love that arises from our inner self as the living response to God's call. Consenting to open ourselves up and to learn to discover deep within ourselves this interior place where we converse with God and wherein we become rich, this is the Reign of God. Our humanity is forever the place of the Divine. With its joys, its weariness, its waiting, its struggles, its sorrows and its sufferings, our life has become the sanctuary of the divine Presence!

From that moment on, according to Clare, each one of us can become "God's assistant," capable of supporting the succumbing members of the "ineffable Body" of God. This "ineffable Body" is the body of our humanity, in the knowledge that in God it now has its foundation, its nobility and its eternity, because the Revelation of God in Jesus Christ cannot be separated from humanity. This is the heart of the Christian mystery: in God's journey through history, in Jesus Christ, God remains with us and, still more deeply, God is in us. In the midst of humanity bending under the weight of sin, misery and sufferings, we are called to become God's collaborators, God's assistants and friends. And it is in that spirit of friendship and total trust, by turning to the Christ whom we bear within, that we become capable of doing good, the good that is Jesus living in us and our living in him. In order to come to that, we have to go through a transformation that Clare, at this point, undertakes to describe.

### *The Transformation to the Divine*

In this letter, Clare invites Agnes to share her spiritual experience: "Place your mind before the mirror of eternity! / Place your soul *in the brilliance of glory*! / Place your heart *in the figure of the* divine *substance*! / And *transform* your entire being *into the image* / of the Godhead Itself through contemplation. / So that you too may feel what His friends feel / as they taste *the hidden sweetness* / that God Himself has reserved from the beginning / for those who love Him." (3 LAg 12–14).

In this invitation to transformation, we can distinguish three stages:

1. At the onset, there is a stop, rest, contemplation: "Place your mind before the mirror of eternity! Place your soul *in the brilliance of glory*!" (3 LAg 12).

In Latin, the term *pono*, translated as "place," means "to fix." For Clare, to contemplate means fixing our gaze on Christ, allowing our eyes to rest firmly on him.

We do not contemplate with our eyes but rather with our mind and our soul. The mind (*mentem*) represents thought. The soul (*anima*) corresponds to our capacity for reflection and understanding.

2. Then comes a movement of the will and the emotions: "Place your heart *in the figure of the* divine

*substance*!" (3 LAg 13).

Here, the heart (*cor*) is the place of feeling.

3. Finally, we come to the stage of pleasure, of delight: "So that you too may feel what His friends feel / as they taste *the hidden sweetness* / that God Himself has reserved from the beginning / for those who love Him" (3 LAg 12–14).

The "sweetness" mentioned by Clare is a "hidden sweetness." It does not allow itself to be grasped immediately. It is not perceptible at once. We are dealing with the sweetness mentioned in the Gospel: throughout the Bible, God has been feeding his people with bread that satisfies every taste and every desire. Thus, God reveals the divine sweetness to a people for whom God is the beloved spouse (Wisdom 16:20–21). The Lord Jesus completes the revelation of this sweetness and gives it to us to taste: "[L]earn from me; for I am gentle and humble in heart" (Matthew 11:29). The Jesus who is saying this is the supreme revelation of the sweetness of God (Matthew 12:18ff.).

In Clare, transformation through contemplation leads to the sweetness of God revealed to God's friends. The path to contemplation that Clare describes involves one's entire being. It includes the intellectual approach of the spirit, the vital and dynamic approach of the soul and the interior vitality of the heart. "Place your mind before the mirror of eternity! / Place your soul *in the brilliance of glory*! / Place your heart *in the figure of the* divine *substance*!" (3 LAg 12–13).

We have to invest the totality of our being in contemplation, all that constitutes the human person: an invitation to stop, fix our attention, to rest in Christ, "the mirror of eternity," "the brilliance of glory," "the figure of the divine substance." The Son reveals the Father who is "eternity," "the glory" and "the divine substance." The application of rest in Christ involves all the divine images of "brilliance" and "glory." This contemplative pause, this rest beside Christ-Mirror, brings about a transformation of our being in the image and the likeness of God: "And *transform* your entire being *into the image* / of the Godhead Itself through contemplation" (3 LAg 13).

To express this notion of transformation to the Divine, Clare draws from Scripture and, in particular, from Saint Paul's epistles: "And all of us, with unveiled faces, seeing the glory of the Lord as though reflected in a mirror, are being transformed into the same image from one degree of glory to another; for this comes from the Lord, the Spirit" (2 Corinthians 3:18).

Clare develops the thought that in contemplating the "brilliance of glory," we are gradually entering into that glory in which we are as though transformed. Here, we are stumbling against the paradox of rest. In fact, a rest that is essentially defined as a state of being static here takes on the mysterious aspect of a dynamic rest in which a transformation to the Divine is taking place. This is achieved in the image of divinity who is Christ, the Son of the Father and, for that very reason, "the mirror of eternity" (3 LAg 12). Here we find ourselves in the presence of the mystery of human beings created in the image and likeness of God (cf. Genesis 1:27).

### *The Spiritual Experience of Love*

Clare is saying that those who love the world, those who love what constitutes the way of the world (the love of money, the race for domination and power) are blind because they do not see the reality that surrounds them. In the next passage, Clare describes the world in a rather negative way. She calls it "deceitful and turbulent." This view of the world corresponds to what she sees and hears around her. In fact, the world that surrounds Clare is highly turbulent, politically and socially: "And, after all who ensnare their blind lovers / in a deceitful and turbulent world / have been completely sent away, / you may totally love Him / Who gave Himself totally for your love, / Whose beauty the sun and the moon admire, / Whose rewards and their preciousness and greatness / are without end; / I am speaking of Him / Who is the Son of the Most High, / Whom the Virgin brought to birth / and remained a virgin after His birth" (3 LAg 15–17).

The revelation of God in Jesus Christ brings about a transformation of our view of the world, of people and of things. In what do we invest our power of loving? Clare invites us to become more deeply rooted in the love of Christ in order to find in him the proper relation with the world around us. It is not a question of "doing" but rather, of receiving a gift, of totally loving "Him Who gave Himself totally."

Clare focuses her attention on God's gift to human beings. God gives himself totally to us (3 LAg 15). The mystery of God is unfathomable but we may approach it through love, self-gift, total self-emptying, so that in turn, we, who are created in God's image and likeness, may renounce ourselves and become love, an infinite gift. Our lives must take the form of being gifts and we must make room for the divine Presence. God is essentially a communion of love. God has no hold over our being except in self-gift. God is He "Who gave Himself totally" out of love for us.

The love of God is resplendent with beauty. This insistence on God's beauty appears when Clare is speaking of love. God's beauty is so extraordinary that even the sun and the moon suspend their course to look at this admirable beauty. God is beautiful. God's beauty surpasses all that we can ever imagine. True beauty opens the way to another conviction that is both vital and gratuitous. The truth of the universe, filled with light, is being revealed beyond the world of power and usefulness. The beauty that Clare describes is beyond what we usually include under this name. Beauty comes from the cross that is full of silence and light.

## *Our Essential Hungers*

Clare vigorously denounces "the enemy of humanity" that seeks to destroy us by generating in us a longing for "the arrogance of momentary and deceptive glories." Such fleeting glory represents the pomp, the glitter and the magnificence that are given to us in life in different forms and that can never satisfy us completely. Clare insists upon the fact that human beings hunger for something other than "momentary glory." There is the hunger of the heart, the need to give ourselves that is stronger than everything else:

> Who would not dread the treacheries of the enemy of humanity who, through the arrogance of momentary and deceptive glories, attempts to reduce to nothing that which is greater than heaven itself? Indeed, it is now clear that the soul of a faithful person, the most worthy of all creatures because of the grace of God, is greater than heaven itself, since the heavens and the rest of creation cannot contain their Creator and only the faithful soul is His dwelling place and throne, and this only through the charity that the wicked lack. [He Who is] the Truth has said: *Whoever loves me will be loved by My Father, and I too shall love him, and We shall come to him and make Our dwelling place with him. . . .* (3 LAg 20–23)

When material hunger, the desire to possess and to control our own lives, other people and things, intensifies in human beings, it can invade the whole area of conscience and thus totally obliterate it. This hunger conceals essential realities. In order to satisfy our desires, we become capable of the best and of the worst. The lure of what we covet can be so strong in us that it leads us to destroy our inmost being, that is, the spiritual hunger that dwells in us.

Thus Clare draws our attention to the indissoluble rapport that exists in us between our material hunger and our spiritual hunger.

### *Believers*

Clare's letters to Agnes show a clear and optimistic view of human beings.

Believers who allow themselves to enter into relationship with God are the greatest of all creatures: This is an extraordinary declaration from Clare. To the degree that we believe, to the degree that we open up to God, God dwells in us. There is something greater than all creatures and this reality, greater than all creatures, is the soul of a faithful person, the soul of a believer: "the most worthy of all creatures because of the grace of God, is greater than heaven itself, since the heavens and the rest of creation cannot contain their Creator and only the faithful soul is His dwelling place and throne, and this only through the charity that the wicked lack" (3 LAg 21–22).

Here Clare's anthropology, the theology dealing with the origin, nature and destiny of human beings, is striking. This image of God in us could give the impression that God is becoming smaller and that somehow we are greater than God. But God's greatness is revealed in God's abasement and, in God's abasement, we have access to real greatness. After having indicated, in a general way, that every believer contains God, Clare specifies the condition—the indispensable relationship of love between God and us, for God to come to dwell in us with the divine mystery. This Johannine theme has a very important place in Clare's spiritual experience: "[He Who is] the Truth has said: *Whoever loves me will be loved by My Father, and I too shall love him, and We shall come to him and make Our dwelling place with him…*" (3 LAg 23).

Here Clare is explicitly quoting John by bringing together two Gospel verses: "those who love me will be loved by my Father, and I will love them and reveal myself to them" (John 14:21), "and we will come to them and make our home with them" (John 14:23).

These two expressions, chosen by Clare, constitute the charter of the Christian spiritual experience. This entire process that tends to contain God spiritually as the Virgin Mary contained him materially leads to this summit: it is not a matter of containing God like an object, as we would keep a treasure in a safe. What is at stake is an interpersonal relationship of love between God and us. This is an astonishing image that surpasses our understanding and all our representations of intimacy. In all human relationships, there is always the unavoidable juxtaposition of two beings who enter into a relationship. Here, however, God is not beside us but, rather, within us, intimately united to us by the closest bond that we can imagine, the bond of love. This is God's dwelling, the plenitude of God, the summit of the theological and spiritual experience. Moreover, all believers are called to such an experience. These are not words reserved to a special group. Instead, they are the promise that God makes to each one of us personally.

### *At the Heart of Human Reality*

There is a striking contrast in Clare between the strength of God's promise and the frailty of this world's transitory promises. By that, Clare means that all we possess on earth will be taken away from us at the time of death. God alone can be possessed for ever:

> As the glorious Virgin of virgins carried [Him] materially, so you, too, *by following in her footprints*...especially [those] of poverty and humility, can, without any doubt, always carry Him spiritually in your chaste and virginal body, holding Him by Whom you and *all things are held together*...possessing that which, in comparison with the other transitory possessions of this world you will possess more securely. How many kings and queens of this world let themselves be deceived, for, even though their pride may reach the skies and their heads touch the clouds, in the end they are as forgotten as a dungheap! (3 LAg 24–28)

As Clare describes it here, the "world" must be understood in the Johannine sense, that is, as the place where the redemption of men and women is accomplished.[3] When Clare refers to the concrete situations of her day, she is thinking of all she sees around her: of some "kings and queens of this world" who, because of their pride, are, as it were, "forgotten as a dung-heap" (3 LAg 27–28).

This terminology may seem difficult to understand. However, if we reflect on its meaning, we perceive a few of the permanent difficulties that confront us. If we are not careful, we can invest our entire being into the glitter of "momentary and deceptive glories" and forget their pernicious and temporal character and then we totally lose ourselves. This is where the "enemy" prevails over us by reducing our lives to a "dung-heap."

Although the world is marked by sin, it is loved by God. In its sin and in spite of its sin, the world is in God's hands. We are at the heart of the realities of the world. They form part of our existence. We should not establish a dualistic rupture between God and the world by escaping into some kind of spiritual abstraction and rejecting the world as something transitory, fleeting and ultimately evil. Such a Gnostic[4] concept is not Christian. From the point of view of faith, the world signifies creation in its unity (origin and end). The world, created for the glory of God, is good, beautiful and meaningful. The world, gratuitously created out of love, is the beneficiary of God's gift: "For God so loved the world that he gave his only Son. . ." (John 3:16).

The presence of Christians in the world implies a responsibility. Believers are invited to bring Christ to the world by living the values of Christ's poverty and humility. Our humanity is saved in Jesus Christ. However, it is advisable for believers to be vigilant with regard to the permanent ambiguity of the world's realities that are marked by the experience of sin.

### *God in Us*

God is hidden in us. But how so? God becomes incarnate in us insofar as we allow him to be visible in our lives. We really become what we are when God is truly visible in our lives, when the face of God can be seen in us. Clare is amazed and in admiration before the fact that "[the One whom] the heavens could not contain, And yet, [the Virgin] carried Him in the little enclosure of her holy womb and held Him on her virginal lap" (3 LAg 18–19). Following the Virgin, believers become the dwelling place of God. They can contain God: "As the glorious Virgin of virgins carried [Him] materially, so you, too, *by following in her footprints*...especially [those] of poverty and humility, can, without any doubt, always carry Him spiritually in your chaste and virginal body, holding Him by Whom you and *all things are held together*...possessing that which, in comparison with the other transitory possessions of this world you will possess more securely" (3 LAg 24–26).

What are the humility and poverty mentioned here? Humility is the calm recognition of reality as it is in us, a broken, incomplete reality with positive and negative aspects. What about poverty? It is the poverty of Jesus, not the poverty of sin, but that of the frailties, the limitations, the capacity to suffer and to die that are inherent in our human condition. For Clare, humility and poverty are closely linked with chastity: "[B]y following in her footprints...especially [those] of poverty and humility, [you] can, without any doubt, always carry Him spiritually in your chaste and virginal body" (3 LAg 25).

When Clare speaks of a "chaste and virginal body," she is alluding to self-control. In us, there is this tragic conflict between what we are and what we do and, at the same time, a constant progress when we become our own masters, a progress that is built up in terms of humanization. Self-control enables us to go to God along our most personal paths and by achieving our own freedom.

Clare is not making a play on words when she explores and presses the following expression: "holding Him by Whom you and all things are held together" (3 LAg 26).

To encounter God and to contain God in ourselves, we have to enter into the divine heart in the biblical and personal sense of the term. This is not interiority cut off from reality, from our own bodies, from other people and from things. We have to come back to that center because it is in the human heart that God sets up his dwelling and it is there that God speaks to us. We have to go down into that center to listen to the Word. We have to go down to that center to look lovingly at others. We have to reach down to that center to find the right relation with things and people. Obviously, this return to the heart does not happen automatically. It implies a whole labor of conversion and, to use traditional terminology, it involves a self-control that we might call ascetic and mystical.

### *Human Beings in Clare's Thought*

Throughout these pages we have sought to understand who human beings are in Clare's thought. In view of the fact that few texts have been preserved and they have a circumstantial aspect, we cannot claim to draw from them her complete view of human beings. However, we cannot deny that Clare's writings reveal a rich and strong view of humanity. For Clare the human body is the marvel of marvels because the absolute and transcendent God entered into the heart of human matter in order to become human. In our insignificance and our poverty, we human beings can contain God! Because the flesh has been glorified in Jesus, the human body is clothed with nobility. This is the reason it is impossible for Clare to think about and meditate on the Incarnation of God in Jesus Christ without better understanding the nobility and the greatness of a single human being and of every human being, without admiring the incomparable sovereignty of the human body having become the sacrament of the divine Presence. Because Clare is attentive to the mystery of human beings, her words on God's mystery are not fruitless.

## *Notes*

[1] This "third letter is from early 1238, when Agnes asked Gregory IX for a new Rule, closer to the kind of life experienced at San Damiano, which the pope refused" (Jean-François Godet, in Claire d'Assise, *Ecrits* [Paris: Editions du Cerf, Coll. "Sources chrétiennes," no. 325, 1985], p. 18).

[2] Francis of Assisi, "True and Perfect Joy," *Francis of Assisi: Early Documents,* Vol. I (New York: New City Press, 1999), pp. 166–167.

[3] "Paul and John have elaborated a theology of salvation history in the world. Because of sin, the present world is evil because it has fallen into the power of the god of the world, the evil one, the prince of this world (Jn 14:30). The world, an ambiguous reality, still bears witness to its Creator (Jn 1:3) but it opposes God by its spirit, its wisdom and its peace: it knows neither God nor Jesus and it hates them (Jn 1:10). But Jesus, sent by God who loves the world, saved the world by conquering it (Jn 3:17). He has taken away the sin of the world (Jn 1:29) by giving his flesh for the world to live (Jn 6:51). The world, structured by sin, is in the process of passing away (1 Cor 7:31); it does not become a 'new cosmos' but it has to be judged and assumed in the kingdom of God (Jn 13:1). Believers have also conquered the world by their faith (1 Jn 5:4 ff.). They undoubtedly remain in this world but, like Jesus, they are no longer of this world (Jn 8:23) and they have to beware of the evil one (Jn 17:15). Thus while shining like stars (Phil 2:15), believers learn how to make good use of this world and they cooperate in its transformation (1 Cor 7:29-31)." (Xavier Léon-Dufour, S.J., "Monde," *Dictionnaire du Nouveau Testament*, p. 375; *Dictionary of the New Testament*, Terrence Prendergast, trans. [New York: Harper & Row, 1980]).

[4] Gnostics were philosophical and religious groups in the second and third centuries A.D. They thought they had an esoteric and initiatory knowledge of religious things, a knowledge allowing them to assure the salvation of human beings and to free them from their bodies. Their doctrine *(gnosis)* is an almost unique attempt at religious salvation in the world through intellectual

knowledge without a direct gift of grace. Creation is cut off from God by a distance that would be insurmountable if a spark of light called *sophia* ("wisdom") did not come to dwell in human beings.

# Part Two

# 'The Poor Christ'

Chapter Four

# 'The Spotless Lamb'

## *The Fourth Letter to Agnes of Prague*[1] *Between February and early August 1253*

[1]To her who is half of her soul and the special shrine of her heart's deepest love, to the illustrious Queen and Bride of the Lamb, the eternal King: to Lady Agnes, her most dear mother, and, of all the others, her favorite daughter, [2]Clare, an unworthy servant of Christ and a *useless* handmaid (Luke 17:10) of His handmaids in the monastery of San Damiano of Assisi: [3]health and [a prayer] that she may she sing *a new song* (Revelation 14:3) with the other most holy virgins before the throne of God and the Lamb and *follow the Lamb wherever He may go* (Revelation 14:4).

[4]O mother and daughter, spouse of the King of all ages, if I have not written to you as often as your soul—and mine as well—desire and long for, do not wonder [5]or think that the fire of love for you glows with less delight in the heart of your mother. [6]No, this is the difficulty: the lack of messengers and the obvious dangers of the roads. [7]Now, however, as I write to your love, I rejoice and exult with you *in the joy of the Spirit* (1 Thessalonians 1:6), O spouse of Christ, [8]because, since you have totally abandoned the vanities of this world, like the other most holy virgin, Saint Agnes, you have been marvelously espoused *to the spotless Lamb, Who takes away the sins of the world* (1 Peter 1:19; John 1:29).

[9]Happy, indeed, is she
to whom it is given to share in this sacred banquet
so that she might cling with all her heart
to Him
[10]Whose beauty all the blessed hosts of heaven
unceasingly admire
[11]Whose affection excites
Whose contemplation refreshes,
Whose kindness fulfills,
[12]Whose delight replenishes,
Whose remembrance delightfully shines,
[13]By whose fragrance the dead are revived,
Whose glorious vision will bless
all the citizens of the heavenly Jerusalem:
[14]which, *since it is the splendor of eternal glory*, is
*the brilliance of eternal light*
*and the mirror without blemish.*

[15]Gaze upon that mirror each day, O Queen and Spouse of Jesus Christ, and continually study your face within it, [16]that you may adorn yourself within and without with beautiful robes, [17]covered, as is becoming the daughter and most chaste bride of the Most High King, with the flowers and garments of all the virtues. [18]Indeed, blessed poverty, holy humility, and inexpressible charity are reflected in that mirror, as, with the grace of God, you can contemplate them throughout the entire mirror.

[19]Look at the border of this mirror, that is, the poverty of Him Who was placed in a manger and wrapped in swaddling clothes.

[20]O marvelous humility!
O astonishing poverty!
[21]The King of angels,
the Lord of heaven and earth,
is laid in a manger!

[22]Then, at the surface of the mirror, consider the holy humility, the blessed poverty, the untold labors and burdens that He endured for the redemption of the whole human race. [23]Then, in the depth of this same mirror, contemplate the ineffable charity that led Him to suffer on the wood of the Cross and to die there the most shameful kind of death.

[24]Therefore,
that Mirror,
suspended on the wood of the Cross,
urged those who passed by to consider, saying:
[25]*"All you who pass by the way,*
*look and see if there is any suffering*
*like my suffering!"*

[26]Let us respond
with one voice,
with one spirit,
to Him crying and grieving Who said:
*"Remembering this over and over*
*leaves my soul downcast within me!"*

[27]From this moment, then, O Queen of our heavenly King, let yourself be inflamed more strongly with the fervor of charity. [28]As you further contemplate His ineffable delights, eternal riches and honors, [29]and sigh for them in the great desire and love of your heart, may you cry out:

[30]*Draw me after you,*
*we will run in the fragrance of your perfumes,*
O heavenly Spouse!
[31]I will run and not tire,
until *You bring me into the wine-cellar,*
[32]until Your *left hand is under my head*
and Your *right hand will embrace me* happily,
[and] *You will kiss me with the* happiest *kiss of Your mouth,*

[33]In this contemplation, may you remember your poor little mother, [34]knowing that *I have inscribed* the happy memory of you *on the tablets of my heart* (Proverbs 3:3), holding you dearer than all the others.

[35]What more can I say? Let the tongue of the flesh be silent when I seek to express my love for you; and let the tongue of the Spirit speak, [36]because the love that I have for you, O blessed daughter, can never be fully expressed by the tongue of the flesh, and even what I have written is an inadequate expression.

[37]I beg you to receive my words with kindness and devotion, seeing in them at least the motherly affection that in the fire of charity I daily feel toward you and your daughters, to whom I warmly commend myself and my daughters in Christ. [38]On their part, these daughters of mine, especially the most prudent virgin Agnes, our sister, recommend themselves in the Lord to you and your daughters.

[39]Farewell, my dearest daughter, to you and your daughters until we meet at the throne *of the glory of the great God* (Titus 2:13), and desire [this] for us.

[40]Inasmuch as I can, I recommend to your charity the bearers of this letter, our dearly beloved Brother Amatus, *beloved of God and men* (Sirach 45:1), and Brother Bonaugura. Amen.

In this letter, written shortly before her death, Clare wanted to say a final word on God to Agnes, a word that she would not have to repeat or rectify, a word that would be transparent enough to allow the light to shine through it. We cannot begin to comment on such a text without truly marveling at everything it offers to our contemplation. With each reading, we see that we will never completely understand it. Each time, like light reflected by a diamond, it has a new, deeper and greater sparkle than we could have imagined. This letter is for all times and all places in the infinity of the Love that Clare sings: a song of the absolute Love who reveals and reflects the absoluteness of Love.

### *'The Lamb, the Eternal King'*

Two groups of names attributed to Christ frame this letter: "The Lamb, the eternal King" and the "mirror without blemish." Between the two, Clare expresses a song, a sort of celebration of nuptial love. The development of the mirror theme, one of the most celebrated in Clare's writings, begins at the end of this text.

Clare refers first to the image of "the Lamb, the eternal King," mentioned in the book of Revelation. She imagines the scene: this vision of the one hundred forty-four thousand on whose foreheads the names of the Lamb and of the Father are written. This is the multitude that follows the Lamb wherever he goes as they sing the new song: a vision of glory and a vision of the future in the eschatological anticipation (Revelation 14:14). The King, whose name appears here, is not a king *among* kings. He is not the king of any particular nation. He is the absolute King, "the Lamb, the eternal King," "the King of all ages." Singing the new song before the throne implies entering into the sanctuary of God, into the Holy of Holies, following the Lamb wherever he goes. Clare sees this new song as the song of deliverance that leads from exile to the kingdom, from what is created to what is infinite and from time to eternity. It is the Easter song, the song of the passage from the created world to the eternity of God.

Jesus is "the spotless Lamb, Who takes away the *sins*[2] of the world." He is the one who saw the evil that generates sin in the reality of human life. Jesus was able to overcome evil because he alone is without sin (John 8:46). He is pure light in which there is no darkness (John 1:5). Clare's thought is in keeping with that perspective: Jesus is not primarily a creature coming from the earth. He is the one who came from above and who is returning above.

In the mystery of Jesus, we not only have a bursting forth of the real attributes of the living and true God but also of the real dimensions of human beings: their greatness as well as their wretchedness. "The Lamb of God" comes to join us in our condition as sinners. Not only does he deliver us from our limitations but he also frees us from the slavery of sin, which intensifies our shackles. Clare writes to Agnes about the way the authentic relationship with God, the relationship of truth between us and God, is a relationship of forgiven sinners to infinite love and mercy: "the poor Crucified, Who for the sake of all of us took upon Himself the Passion of the Cross . . . delivered us from the power of the Prince of Darkness . . . to whom we were enslaved because of the disobedience of our first parent, and so reconciled us to God the Father" (1 LAg 13–14).

### *Admiration*

"The immaculate Lamb" evokes the admiration of all the blessed hosts of heaven. His "glorious vision will bless all the citizens of the heavenly Jerusalem" since his beauty "is the splendor of eternal glory. . . the brilliance of eternal light and the mirror without blemish" (4 LAg 10, 13–14). The contemplative experience that is described here is emotion, rapture and delight. In this context, admiration is not the outcome but an approach, an openness to this inexpressible supreme beauty. There does not seem to be a better prayer. The beauty, evoked here in a dazzling way, is God himself. Clare attempts to say who God is for her in symbolic language, the language of mystery. How can she do it since she is speaking of the "splendor of eternal glory"? Clare imagines a whole variety of terms most likely to evoke the inexpressible being. Beauty is the name of the One Clare loves and she uses that to name him. The immaculate Lamb is the only one. He is forever the incarnation of absolute beauty for Clare.

## *Intelligence, Will and Contemplation*

The contemplation of the immaculate Lamb consists in deeply penetrating into the beauty of his face to come closer to what he truly is. Moving beyond this face engages the will and intelligence that make up our inmost being. Without the will, we are not in an attitude of contemplation.

The doctrine of the spiritual senses, elaborated in Clare's writings, has its origin in patristic literature and, most especially, in Saint Augustine. After Origen, Augustine was considered the master of the theology of the Middle Ages in this field. Clare is following the same line as that of the twelfth-century mystics: Bernard of Clairvaux, William of Saint-Thierry, Aelred of Rievaulx and those of the so-called high scholastic period, such as William of Auxerre, William of Auvergne, Alexander of Hales, Albert the Great, Anthony of Padua, Thomas Aquinas and Bonaventure.

Karl Rahner showed that, after the patristic period, it was only at the height of scholasticism that, once again, there was rich and original thinking about the spiritual senses. In an article on the doctrine of the spiritual senses in the Middle Ages,[3] he develops this thought, especially in relation to the mystical theology of Saint Bonaventure.[4] In Bonaventure's view, those who attain peace, the state of spiritual enjoyment, have arrived at the threshold of contemplation. In that case, this contemplation is established through the activities of the spiritual senses.

In all likelihood, Clare of Assisi was influenced by Bonaventure's doctrine of the five senses. In her writings, we find the same functions of the senses as in Bonaventure: Sight and hearing are closely connected with intelligence. Taste, smell and touch are linked to the will. In contemplation of the feelings, Clare describes what takes place when we come in contact with Love: "Happy, indeed, is she / to whom it is given to share in this sacred banquet / so that she might cling with all her heart / to Him / Whose beauty all the blessed hosts of heaven unceasingly admire / Whose affection excites / Whose contemplation refreshes, / Whose kindness fulfills, / Whose delight replenishes, / Whose remembrance delightfully shines" (4 LAg 9–12).

Here a human being should be perceived as a whole, in harmony with the world and in relationship with God. Created in God's image, we do not have bodies that are dissociated from our experience of God and souls that can move forward to divine depths. Instead, the whole person, body and soul, experiences God. In this contemplation, intelligence has its place: the memory of the Lamb "delightfully shines" in the spirit of those who contemplate him. The verb "to shine," a literal translation of the Latin *lucere*, should be understood in the sense of lighting, illuminating and even burning. The memory of the Lamb shines brightly in the spirit. Like a glowing fire, his memory burns softly in our memory. The thought of the Lamb leaves the trace of a burn on the intelligence. Here love rejoins faith. In other words, for Clare, contemplation is the leap of faith, a leap toward God in whom our entire being becomes one. In fact, it is after this contemplation that Clare's faith in the Risen Christ is expressed: "By Whose fragrance the dead are revived, / Whose glorious vision will bless / all the citizens of the heavenly Jerusalem" (4 LAg 13).

Here we are dealing with the physical and spiritual resurrection that will take place on the last day (Revelation 21:1–4), symbolized by the "fragrance" of the Risen one, the "firstborn of the dead" (Revelation 1:5). The fragrance of the Risen Christ will revive the dead: the perfume of his burial has been spreading throughout the world from the moment his body that had been broken by death and anointed by his own, was raised to life again. The resurrection of the dead, foretold by Scripture (1 Corinthians 15:4), has been accomplished in Christ.

As to the spiritual resurrection, it is presented as a "glorious vision." It is the vision of the Lamb (4 LAg 10). Henceforth, the victorious Christ, "the spotless Lamb," illumines "those who sit in darkness / and in the shadow of death" (Luke 1:79). However, it is at the end of time, at the Parousia,[5] that his triumph will reach its highest fulfillment at the general resurrection. This is why Clare uses the future: his "glorious vision will bless / all the citizens of the heavenly Jerusalem" (4 LAg 13). Clare is already seeing the dazzlingly bright new Jerusalem coming down out of heaven: "[T]he glory of God is its light, and its lamp is the Lamb" (Revelation 21:23). From the light of the day that alternates here on earth with the shadow of the night, the redeemed of the earth will forever enter into the never-fading light that is God himself (1 John 1:5).

### *The Unified Being*

When Clare speaks of clinging "with all her heart / to Him / Whose beauty all the blessed hosts of heaven unceasingly admire" (4 LAg 9–10), it is not merely a vision involving only our intelligence, our will and our memory. We are dealing with the unification of the whole human being, body and soul. We have already seen how the will (affectivity, or emotion) plays an essential part: it is the spring of desire. However, contemplation is not limited to vision. Other senses—taste and smell—participate in this approach. We have to understand contemplation as a transformation, a fulfillment and union of our being. From this perspective, we discover divine beauty. This experience of beauty captivates us. The locus of our desire, it generates in us the fundamental movement that opens us up to something else. This openness is the space of God. At this point, our existence becomes turned to beauty. Through communion with the beauty of God, we are experiencing the encounter with Otherness. Beauty, the presence of an unfathomable call that strips us, places us in contact with our lowliness and our poverty.

The experience of beauty enables us to reach Someone who is greater than we are. We have to go further still in Clare's thought to move forward to the discovery of this mystery.

Clare describes Christ as "more beautiful than the children of men." She admonishes her reader to "contemplate [Him]," who "became, for your salvation, the lowest of men, was despised, struck, scourged untold times thoughout His entire body, and then died amid the suffering of the Cross" (2 LAg 20).

Here, we find the suggestion of the description of the suffering servant depicted in the book of Isaiah: "so marred was his appearance, / beyond human semblance. ... [H]e had no form or majesty that we should look at him, / nothing in his appearance that we should desire him. / He was despised and rejected by others; / a man of suffering and acquainted with infirmity; / and as one from whom others hide their faces / he was despised, and we held him of no account" (Isaiah 52:14; 53:2–3).

What is the particular beauty of God that allows a face as marred as that of the crucified Christ was on the day of his Passion to be seen by Clare as the face of one "more beautiful than the children of men" (2 LAg 20), "the splendor of eternal glory... the brilliance of eternal light ... and the mirror without blemish" (4 LAg 14)?

## *Notes*

[1] This "fourth letter dates from the beginning of 1253: it was written by Clare after the return to San Damiano of her sister [by blood] Agnes [early 1253], and before her own death [on August 11, 1253]" (Jean-François Godet, in Claire D'Assise, *Ecrits* [Paris: Editions du Cerf, Coll. "Sources chrétiennes," no. 325, 1985], p. 18).

[2] 4 LAg 8, in her letter written to Agnes, Clare does use the plural form: *"Agno immaculato, qui tollit peccata mundi"* ("the

Immaculate Lamb who takes away the sins of the world," ECl, pp. 112–113).

[3] Karl Rahner, "The Doctrine of the 'Spiritual Senses' in the Middle Ages (especially in St. Bonaventure)," *Theological Investigations*, Vol. XVI, pp. 263–299.

[4] "According to St. Bonaventure, the soul in the state of grace has a threefold *habitus* (state): the *habitus* of virtues, the *habitus* of the gifts of the Holy Spirit and the *habitus* of the beatitudes. Through these three *habitus*, the powers of the soul are rectified, their activity is made easier, they develop and they are strengthened and finally, they are brought to the perfection that human beings cannot attain on this earth. Although these three *habitus* are necessarily given with the state of grace, their activity, however, is not exercised at the same time. Rather, each one of them corresponds to one of the three stages of the spiritual life: beginning (purification), progress (illumination) and perfecting. If people who have attained perfection also avail themselves of the sevenfold *habitus* of the beatitudes, they enter into a state of profound peace" (*Ibid.*, p. 271).

[5] The term "Parousia" is from the Greek, meaning "presence" or "arrival." In the New Testament the term is used to designate Christ's glorious return at the end of time.

CHAPTER FIVE

# 'The Mirror without Blemish'

Throughout the poem she had just written, Clare was speaking of the "mirror" without explicitly naming it. Now that she has named it, Clare will not let go of this new image in speaking of Christ. This is one of the most famous passages in her writings:

> Happy, indeed, is she / to whom it is given to share in this sacred banquet / so that she might cling with all her heart / to Him / Whose beauty all the blessed hosts of heaven unceasingly admire / By whose fragrance the dead are revived, / Whose glorious vision will bless / all the citizens of the heavenly Jerusalem: / which, *since it is the splendor of eternal glory,* is / *the brilliance of eternal light / and the mirror without blemish.*
>
> Gaze upon that mirror each day, O Queen and Spouse of Jesus Christ, and continually study your face within it, that you may adorn yourself within and without with beautiful robes, covered, as is becoming the daughter and most chaste bride of the Most High King, with the flowers and garments of all the virtues. Indeed, blessed poverty, holy humility, and inexpressible charity are reflected in that mirror, as, with the grace of God, you can contemplate them throughout the entire mirror.
>
> Look at the border of this mirror, that is, the poverty of Him Who was placed in a manger and wrapped in swaddling clothes.

O marvelous humility! / O astonishing poverty! / The King of angels, / the Lord of heaven and earth, / is laid in a manger!

Then, at the surface of the mirror, consider the holy humility, the blessed poverty, the untold labors and burdens that He endured for the redemption of the whole human race. Then, in the depth of this same mirror, contemplate the ineffable charity that led Him to suffer on the wood of the Cross and to die there the most shameful kind of death.

Therefore, / that Mirror, / suspended on the wood of the Cross, / urged those who passed by to consider, saying: / "*All you who pass by the way, / look and see if there is any suffering / like my suffering*!" / Let us respond / with one voice, / with one spirit, / to Him crying and grieving Who said: / "*Remembering this over and over / leaves my soul downcast within me*!"

From this moment, then, O Queen of our heavenly King, let yourself be inflamed more strongly with the fervor of charity. As you further contemplate His ineffable delights, eternal riches and honors, and sigh for them in the great desire and love of your heart, may you cry out:

*Draw me after you,/ we will run in the fragrance of your perfumes,*

O heavenly Spouse! / I will run and not tire, / until *You bring me into the wine-cellar,* / until Your *left hand is under my head* / and Your *right hand will embrace me* happily, / [and] *You will kiss me with the* happiest *kiss of Your mouth.* (4 LAg 9-10; 13–32)

### *The Symbolism of the Mirror*

In his book, *Reflets dans le miroir (Reflections in the Mirror)*, Brian E. Purfield describes the spiritual context of the lives of Clare and Francis of Assisi. He explains how the theme of the mirror, already present in Scripture (Wisdom 7:26), is also found both in sacred and secular literature of Clare's time. Purfield examines the use and importance of the mirror image in the Middle Ages and in Clare's writings. This study enables us to discover how the theme developed from the figurative meaning it might have had in ancient times and in the Middle Ages to the significant meaning of the mirror in Clare's writing:

> The theme of the mirror, in relation to the theme of God's image, is one of the most fascinating themes in spiritual literature. In classical times, Plato and Plotinus dealt with the soul as a mirror. The apostle Paul used this symbol to characterize the faith of Christians and their vision of God. For many mystics, the mirror is the very emblem of their contemplation.
>
> In her letters, Saint Clare of Assisi developed this theme several times and added new elements to the tradition. She insists on the mediating role of Christ, who reveals God-Trinity to us and, following that, Jesus' entire life unfolds before her eyes in the mirror. Clare reminds us that contemplation is not a mere reflection but, rather, it is a participation and a transformation of the beholder. She emphasizes that, as they are being transformed, Christians, in turn, have to become mirrors and to reflect God.[1]

In trying to express our most profound experiences, we use images and symbols that go beyond their literal meaning. Clare chose the symbolism of the mirror to embody her approach to the mystery of Christ. We cannot comprehend the theme of the mirror in Clare if we do not keep in mind that the light, the expression of the presence of God, is what enlivens it. This mirror is the form, that is, the structure in which Clare found the semantic space to express who is the God who is manifested in Jesus Christ. In this mirror, Clare strives to move from what is visible to the Invisible, from what is known to the Unknown. In this mirror, our image, the image of humankind, is reflected in the image of God. Thus, we enter into a three-part relationship, that of God, Jesus Christ and human beings.

With a series of images and arguments arousing our senses, Clare leads us in stages to enter into the symbolism of the mirror and helps us to discover the truth of God. First, Clare speaks of the mirror as an ordinary mirror in which we appear to ourselves in our full radiance. Yet, it is not an ordinary mirror to be used for preening, for she moves us toward inward transformation. In this mirror, we become centered through recovering our exterior and interior harmony.

> Gaze upon that mirror each day, O Queen and Spouse of Jesus Christ, and continually study your face within it, that you may adorn yourself within and without with beautiful robes, covered, as is becoming the daughter and most chaste bride of the Most High King, with the flowers and garments of all the virtues. Indeed, blessed poverty, holy humility, and inexpressible charity are reflected in that mirror, as, with the grace of God, you can contemplate them throughout the entire mirror.
> (4 LAg 15–18)

When we contemplate that mirror, we are made more beautiful, we are marvelously clothed,[2] adorned by all sorts of varied fabrics. These garments are not ordinary clothes, but the virtues of Christ that appear on the mirror: "blessed poverty, holy humility, and inexpressible charity" (4 LAg 18).

Who does not remember the myth of Narcissus who fell in love with his own image reflected in a pool? This myth helps us to understand a profound truth about the human condition. We all have a more beautiful image of ourselves than the real one. We all harbor an image of ourselves as the human ideal.

"The mirror without blemish" that Clare speaks of is the very opposite of Narcissus's mirror. As human beings, our profound mystery does not rest in the idealized image that we project to ourselves but, instead, in the image of

God in whose likeness we were created. As we contemplate "the mirror of eternity," we are called to become transformed and to make ours the poverty, the humility and the love radiated by the image of the Divinity, an image that Clare leads us to glimpse in "the mirror without blemish." This mirror is a Someone. We have to know God manifested in Jesus Christ and we have to enter into his mystery. And since we are dealing with God in person, there is no other way to know God, to see God in his light than by communion with God through a life of light. It is in the light that we see the Light.

### *'Border . . . Surface . . . Depth'*

The mirror is described as being made up of three parts, each representing the events of the life of Jesus:

> Look at the border of this mirror, that is, the poverty of Him Who was placed in a manger and wrapped in swaddling clothes.
>
> O marvelous humility! / O astonishing poverty! / The King of angels, / the Lord of heaven and earth, / is laid in a manger!
>
> Then, at the surface of the mirror, consider the holy humility, the blessed poverty, the untold labors and burdens that He endured for the redemption of the whole human race. Then, in the depth of this same mirror, contemplate the ineffable charity that led Him to suffer on the wood of the Cross and to die there the most shameful kind of death. (4 LAg 19-23)

"The border" of the mirror corresponds to the birth of Jesus, "the surface" refers to his life on earth and "the depth," to the death of Christ on the cross. Here is a suggestion of a progression of spiritual life, a movement forward in the knowledge of God. This contemplation excludes all static representation of God since the spiritual knowledge is like a perpetual and amazing discovery.

### *'At the Border of This Mirror'*

At the border, at the start of Jesus' life, we have to consider the destitution of the One who was laid in a manger and so miserably clothed: "Look at the border of this mirror, that is, the poverty of Him Who was placed in a manger and wrapped in swaddling clothes. / O marvelous humility! / O astonishing poverty! / The King of angels, / the Lord of heaven and earth, / is laid in a manger!" (4 LAg 19–21).

Our eyes are turned completely to this border, or beginning, when the Lord entered into our history: "The King of angels, the Lord of heaven and earth" is laid[3] there in a manger. We have to consider the greatness of his humility manifested in the abasement of the Incarnation. That which radiates in the manger is a marvelous teaching. God is adapting to us by accepting embodiment in fragile humankind. This is the first teaching of sacred Scripture.

Clare keeps alive this memory of the poverty of the manger. Thomas of Celano is fond of recalling it: "She encouraged [her sisters] in their little nest of poverty / to be conformed to the poor Christ, / Whom a poor Mother placed as an infant in a narrow crib. / With this special reminder, / as if with a jewel of gold, / she adorned her breast, / so that no speck of the dust of earthly things would enter her."[4]

Clare discovers the face of God there in the poverty of the manger. The Incarnation manifests in time and space to what extent humility is at the heart of divine glory and shows that God's infinity is an infinity of humility. For Clare's contemplation does not stop at the face of Christ. Her gaze goes beyond. In the radiance of the mirror of Christ, she perceives the eternal light of the Father. She looks at "the Icon of the invisible God" as Saint Paul suggests in his letter to the Colossians: "He is the image of the invisible God, the firstborn of all creation; for in him all things in heaven and on earth were created, things visible and invisible, whether thrones or dominions or rulers or powers—all things have been created through him and for him" (Colossians 1:15–16).

The border of the "mirror" reveals that God is infinite poverty, supreme emptying. God is God in our midst in the infinitely precious and fragile face of an infant who calls and entreats us.

The concrete poverty of the manger causes amazement and astonishment. In discovering what is unique in this mirror, Clare moves from words to silence and from silence to words. In the presence of the unfathomable mystery of God manifested in the poverty of the manger, she marvels: "O marvelous humility! / O astonishing poverty! / The King of angels, / the Lord of heaven and earth is laid in a manger!" (4 LAg 20–21).

### *'At the Surface of the Mirror'*

The whole reality of the divine being is manifested in the life of Jesus: "[A]t the surface of the mirror, consider the holy humility, the blessed poverty, the untold labors and burdens that He endured for the redemption of the whole human race" (4 LAg 22).

Elsewhere in her Testament, Clare expresses her love for "the God Who was placed poor in the crib, lived poor in the world, and remained naked on the cross" (TCl 45). God awaits us in the concrete life of Jesus. God awaits us in the humility and the poverty of his failure. God awaits us in the opprobrium and the ignominy of the "untold labors and burdens that He endured for the redemption[5] of the whole human race." Here is authentic salvation, the inversion of all that we expected, the inversion of all our dreams about God: our redemption is in the apparent defeat of Christ's life, in the weakness, the indigence and poverty of his existence. Nothing in the world can make us more human, nothing can purify us more deeply than to listen to this life of Jesus for "the truth is that only in the mystery of the Incarnate Word does the mystery of man take on light."[6] Jesus' entire earthly life seeks to lead us on this path of dispossession that leads to life. Humility is not an inferiority complex or prostration before God. It is the return to the humus,[7] the return to our proper human place on earth. Clare develops this humanizing spirituality. She invites us to enter into this *kenosis*,[8] to rejoin the Lord at the heart of history. This *kenosis* invites us to accept the weakness of a humble and poor God who took on our condition so that we would have a new sense of humanity and of God, so that we would bring to all our brothers and sisters and to all those we encounter, this wordless revelation of a greatness that consists in putting on humility for God's life to be manifested.

### *'In the Depth of the Mirror'*

To this point, Clare has used the verbs *attendere* ("to be attentive," "to listen") and *considerare* ("to examine with care and respect") that we translate "to consider" or "to look" to lead us to the discovery of the mirror: "Look at [*attendere*] the border of this mirror, that is, the poverty of Him Who was placed in a manger and wrapped in swaddling clothes" (4 LAg 19). "Then, at the surface of the mirror, consider [*considerare*] the holy humility, the blessed poverty, the untold labors and burdens that He endured for the redemption of the whole human race" (4 LAg 22).

Now Clare uses the word *contemplare* ("to look at attentively"), that we translate as "to contemplate." "Then, in the depth of this same mirror, contemplate [*contemplare*] the ineffable charity that led Him to suffer on the wood of the Cross and to die there the most shameful kind of death" (4 LAg 23).

Clare proposes we enter into contemplation in the way we understand it today. The point is to meditate attentively on what is most important: "the ineffable charity" of the "poor Christ." In Clare's thinking, poverty and humility are always interrelated and they lead us to discover love that is the very being of God. For her, only the love of God, manifested in Jesus Christ, shines in the mirror: "blessed poverty, holy humility and inexpressible charity are reflected[9] in that mirror" (4 LAg 18).

God is love. Love is God himself. We have to concentrate our gaze on this love manifested in the humility and the poverty of Jesus' life. Clare expresses her fascination with Christ's humanity by considering the different images of his poverty and humility. The different parts of the mirror relating the life of Christ amaze and astonish Clare. To capture the richness of her teaching through this symbol of faith that is the mirror of Christ's virtues, not only do we have to consider attentively the "poverty" and the "humility" of Christ but also "the ineffable charity"of the One who has loved us. The first two virtues would be meaningless if they were not supported by love. Christ loved humankind to the extreme point of the agony of death, even death on a cross. Encountering and following Jesus means entering into this abyss of suffering and death where love finds its supreme fulfillment. The mystery of Jesus' Passion can open up unexpected horizons for us. As we enter into the depths of silence, suffering and death, allowing Christ's love to develop in us without adding anything to it, we discover another face of God. The revelation of this face cannot be expressed in words because there is nothing greater. According to Clare, true contemplation consists precisely in discovering the wonder of the love whereby God considers our lives at the cost of his own life.

### *The Beauty of Love*

It is clear that the beauty of God, manifested in the Passion and the death of Christ, is the beauty that bursts from within love. Love imprints beauty on the marred face of the poor Christ. If Christ's sufferings on the cross can horrify us, if hatred can take on such a dreadful aspect, it is because of the obscure forces of evil seeking to destroy God's work in the universe. Here silence is indispensable, a silence made of listening at the heart of darkness where we encounter divine love calling and entreating us. The real encounter with Christ occurs precisely where his face, marred by suffering, appears in all its truth. And beauty is born of truth. It is there, in silence and contemplation, that we can encounter Christ when an infinite and unforgettable light passes from the depths of his being into the depths of ours. It is there that we can rejoin Christ at the center of the world, at the foot of the cross, to welcome his weakness and his frailty: "Therefore, / that Mirror, / suspended on the wood of the Cross, / urged those who passed by to consider, saying: / *'All you who pass by this way, / look and see if there is any suffering / like my suffering!'*" (4 LAg 24–25).

In putting on the flesh of our weak humanity, Jesus experienced hunger for all who hunger, thirst for all who thirst. He suffered in all those who are suffering and he endured death in all those who are dying. Believing in a God who suffers only enhances the mystery.

### *The Burning Flame of Love*

"Let us respond / with one voice, / with one spirit, / to Him crying and grieving Who said: / 'Remembering this over and over / leaves my soul downcast within me'" (4 LAg 26).

For Clare, the purpose of contemplation is to reach God by the power of human desire that has its source in human emotion.

An existential knowledge of God presupposes a certain disposition and experience of our interior senses. In terms of the changes that affect our memory, God can take on particular aspects. Clare gives different names to

Christ. She calls him "the Lamb, the eternal King" or "the spotless Lamb," "the splendor of eternal glory" or "the brilliance of eternal light" or again "the mirror without blemish." The variousness of his unchangeable nature is not at stake but, rather, the multiple changes of emotion linked to the movements of the soul. This is neither a corporal phenomenon nor a fabrication of the imagination. It is, instead, a spiritual union whereby the Lord is welcomed with feelings of love as the one who loves tenderly. This is why we are invited to respond to this call: "From this moment, then, O Queen of our heavenly King, let yourself be inflamed more strongly with the fervor of charity" (4 LAg 27).

Love appears in the form of fire: "let yourself be inflamed." The thought of Christ burns the heart. For Clare, there is no contemplative activity that does not involve the emotion in one way or another. In this context, our capacity for enjoyment is important because spiritual life presupposes the possibility of being drawn by the One we love. Contemplating means enjoying the indescribable delights, riches and everlasting honors of Christ as we sigh with desire and love. The verb "to sigh" evokes the image of breath. It is also an image of love. To contemplate is to sigh as we wait for the Beloved and long for him. "As you further contemplate His ineffable delights, eternal riches and honors, and sigh for them in the great desire and love of your heart, may you cry out: *Draw me after you, / we will run in the fragrance of your perfumes, /* O heavenly Spouse!" (4 LAg 28–30).

### *The Love Race*

In a song inspired by the Song of Solomon, Clare celebrates mystical love. Here, the language becomes even more vivid, more forceful and more filled with images. The presence of the Beloved inflames; the fragrance of his perfumes is sweet. The race implied in these verses is a movement that would be called *accelerando*[10] in music. After having chosen the path of most holy poverty, in a spirit of great humility and most fervent charity, Clare started to walk on that path mindful to remain faithful to the path of Christ. And now this walk has become a race because of the great freedom she experiences. This path flows into "the breadth and length and height and depth" of love (Ephesians 3:18) like God's grace and generosity. In the language of the Song of Solomon, this fervor becomes haste. The bride does not approach the Bridegroom slowly. She runs madly toward him then, carried away by her own haste, she lovingly exclaims: "Draw me after you, / we will run in the fragrance of your perfumes, / O heavenly Spouse!" (4 LAg 30).

The perfume lingers and draws the running bride, who "will run and not tire."

The theme of the race indicates the buoyancy of a righteous life, adding a note of fidelity and perseverance in which there is no room for fatigue or weariness. In another letter, Clare had written:

> But because *one thing is necessary*... I bear witness to that one thing and encourage you, for love of Him to Whom you have offered yourself as *a holy* and pleasing *sacrifice*... that you always be mindful of your resolution like another Rachel always seeing your beginning....
>
> What you hold, may you [always] hold, / What you do, may you [always] do and never abandon. / But with swift pace, light step, / unswerving feet, / so that even your steps stir up no dust, / may you go forward securely, joyfully, and swiftly, / on the path of prudent happiness, / not believing anything, / not agreeing with anything / that would dissuade you from this resolution / or that would place a stumbling block for you on the way, / so that you may offer your vows to the Most High / in the pursuit of that perfection / to which the Spirit of the Lord has called you. (2 LAg 10–14)

### *'The Happiest Kiss'*

Profound spiritual life can only be expressed in the language of love because we are touching upon the fundamental human experience. The loving contemplation deepens until the Bride, Clare says, is led to "the wine-cellar" (4 LAg 31; Song of Solomon 2:4 [NRSV: 'the banqueting house']). "The wine-cellar" contains the reserves, the royal treasures of the Bridegroom. They delight, nourish and fortify. Their enjoyment, the source of life, is felt in the depths of our being.

The mystery of love is accomplished. The union of the lovers takes place in the indissoluble union of love: "I will run and not tire, / until You bring me into the wine-cellar, / until Your left hand is under my head / and Your right hand will embrace me happily, / [and] You will kiss me with the happiest kiss of Your mouth" (4 LAg 31–32). This union is an embrace, an abyss, a dream, a secret, a delight and a happiness beyond words. It is the union in eternity of the Bridegroom and the Bride, the amorous embrace, the mystical interchange of knowledge and rapture: "and you will kiss me with the happiest kiss of Your mouth" (4 LAg 32). The exterior and loving union of the bodies, the kiss, is the sign of the interior union. That kiss instills a personal and exclusive joy bathed in love. The triumph of love is accomplished in a kiss that expresses the ardent and imperishable wish of love: that the couple be forever one in an indissoluble and eternal union.

### *God's Love as the Source of All Relationships*

One with Christ in this contemplation, Clare expresses her affection for Agnes of Prague in terms of fire:

> In this contemplation, may you remember your poor little mother, knowing that *I have inscribed* the happy memory of you *on the tablets of my heart*... holding you dearer than all the others.

> What more can I say? Let the tongue of the flesh be silent when I seek to express my love for you; and let the tongue of the Spirit speak, because the love that I have for you, O blessed daughter, can never be fully expressed by the tongue of the flesh, and even what I have written is an inadequate expression.
>
> I beg you to receive my words with kindness and devotion, seeing in them at least the motherly affection that in the fire of charity I daily feel toward you and your daughters, to whom I warmly commend myself and my daughters in Christ. (4 LAg 33–37)

We often tend to believe that once we are immersed in a profound contemplation of Jesus Christ, God and his mystery, we will forget everything else. However, here the opposite is expressed. In Clare's thought, the contemplation of God's love sends us back to our love relationships. The first love will always have to strive to expand to relationships with our brothers and sisters. We might add that it is by expanding these relationships that God's love gives its full measure and shows its true nature by never being closed in upon itself. If one or another of our relationships reaches such a depth as to indicate the boundless love of God, does it perhaps then fulfill Christ's longing? We have a vivid example of this in the spiritual friendship of Clare and Agnes in which the most genuine divine love is manifested.

## *Notes*

[1] Brian E. Purfield, *Reflets dans le miroir. Images du Christ dans la vie spirituelle de sainte Claire d'Assise* (Paris: Editions franciscaines, 1993), back cover. Translation by Colette Joly Dees. This work appeared first in English as *Reflections in the Mirror: Images of Christ in the Spiritual Life of Saint Clare of Assisi* (1989), a dissertation at St. Bonaventure University, St. Bonaventure, New York.

[2] In the sense that Saint-Exupéry uses the terms to speak of "dressing up the heart" when we encounter a friend: "If, for example, you come at four in the afternoon, I will start to be happy at three. The closer the time approaches, the happier I will be. At four, I will already become excited and I will worry. I will discover the price of happiness! But if you come at any time at all, I will never know when to dress up my heart..." (Antoine de Saint-Exupéry, *Le Petit Prince*, ch. 21, pp. 69–70; *The Little Prince*, Katherine Woods, trans. [San Diego: Harcourt Brace & Co., 1993]).

[3] 4 LAg 19, 24; ECl., pp. 114–115. *Ponere* ("to lay") is the Latin verb used in the original text. For Clare, Jesus has been laid in a manger just as he will be laid on the cross. "*Attende, inquam, principium huius speculi paupertatem positi siquidem in praesepio et in panniculis involuti*" ("Look at the border of this mirror, that is, the poverty of Him Who was placed in a manger and wrapped in swaddling clothes") (4 LAg 19). "*Unde ipsum speculum, in ligno crucis positum, hic consideranda transeuntes monebat dicens...*" ("Therefore, / that Mirror, / suspended on the wood of the Cross, / urged those who passed by to consider...") (4 LAg 24).

[4] Thomas of Celano, "The Legend of Saint Clare," Part I, 13, "Her Holy and Sincere Poverty," ED, p. 269.

[5] This word, that means "buying back," owes its origin to its use in trading. In the religious sense, redemption evokes the idea of salvation: Jesus liberates humankind from slavery.

[6] Encyclical letter *Redemptor hominis*, 1979, no. 8, "Redemption as a New Creation."

[7] From the Latin *humus*, "earth."

[8] This Greek term designates the action by which we empty something or ourselves. In biblical theology, this term is used to express Christ's self-emptying in the Incarnation, in his obedience to the Father and in his deliberate acceptance of death (Philippians 2:6–11). For Christ in his earthly life, *kenosis* signified his renouncing the manifestation of the glory he had from his Father.

[9] 4 LAg 18, ECl, pp. 114–115. The verb "reflected" (*resplendeo*) is in the singular in the original Latin: "*In hoc autem speculo refulget beata paupertas, sancta humilitas et ineffabilis caritas*" ("In this mirror, blessed poverty, holy humility and ineffable charity are also reflected").

[10] This Italian word means "to accelerate," "to go faster."

CHAPTER SIX

# The Christ of Clare

For Clare, Jesus is the *Christ,* "the anointed."[1] This title, taken from Scripture, recalls the Old Testament anointing[2] that confers royal power on a man (1 Kings 19:16). In the New Testament, it designates God's Anointed, Jesus Christ, who is entrusted with the royal, priestly and prophetic ministry (Hebrews 1:8 ff.). We find the names "King" and "Son" attributed to Christ in the following writings:

—"The King" (2 LAg 5); "the Most High King of heaven" (3 LAg 1); "the Lamb, the eternal king" (4 LAg 1); "the King of all ages" (4 LAg 4); "the Most High King" (4 LAg 17); "the King of angels" (4 LAg 21); "heavenly King" (4 LAg 27).

—"The Son" (BCl 1); "the Son of the Most High Father" (1 LAg 24); "Son whom the heavens could not contain" (3 LAg 18); "the Son of God" (TCl 5, 35); "the Beloved Son" (TCl 46).

Clare adds other titles to the two just mentioned:

—"The Lord"[3]: "the Lord of heaven and earth" (4 LAg 21).

—"The Lamb"[4]:"the Lamb, the eternal King" (4 LAg 1); "the spotless Lamb, who takes away the sins of the world" (4 LAg 8).

—"The Creator": "the Lord Jesus Christ / Who ruled and now rules heaven and earth, / Who spoke and things were made" (1 LAg 17); "by Whom all things have been made from nothing" (3 LAg 7); the "Creator" "the heavens and the rest of creation cannot contain" (3 LAg 22).

—"The Eternal One": "the Lamb, the eternal King" (4 LAg 1); "the King of all ages" (4 LAg 4); *"the splendor of eternal glory," "the brilliance of eternal light"* (4 LAg 14); "the mirror of eternity" (3 LAg 12).

To these various names, Clare attributes glory, power, light, beauty, splendor and greatness:

—"He is seated in glory on a starry throne" (2 LAg 5).

—"The Lord Jesus Christ" is the one whose "power is stronger, / Whose generosity more abundant, / Whose appearance more beautiful, / Whose love more tender, / Whose courtesy more gracious" (1 LAg 9, 17).

—"The Son" is *"more beautiful than the children of men"* (2 LAg 20), the one "Whose beauty the sun and the moon admire" (3 LAg 16).

—"The Lamb, the eternal King," *"the spotless Lamb, Who takes away the sins of the world"* (4 LAg 8) is the one "Whose beauty all the blessed hosts of heaven unceasingly admire . . . *since it is the splendor of eternal glory, is the brilliance of eternal light and the mirror without blemish"* (4 LAg 10, 14).[5]

—"The Creator," "Who spoke and things were made" came "into the Virgin's womb" (1 LAg 17, 19); "the heavens and the rest of creation cannot contain their Creator and only the faithful soul is His dwelling place and throne" (3 LAg 22).

—"[T]he mirror of eternity" (3 LAg 12) is *"the mirror without blemish"* (4 LAg 14).

The striking contrast of the words that express the mystery of Jesus Christ is a characteristic element of Clare's theological thought. Clare never dwells exclusively on the majestic Christ. He also appears to her as "the poor Christ" (2 LAg 18), that is, the glorious One lowered himself to poverty and suffering throughout his earthly life: he was born poor, he lived and died poor (TCl 45). However, he remains today and forever, "the Lamb, the eternal King" (4 LAg 1), "the Lord of heaven and earth" (4 LAg 21). Clare keeps the balance between the divinity and the humanity of the One she loves to call "the poor Christ" (2 LAg 18).

### *Christ Made Himself Poor*

The Christ of Clare took on our human condition, making this a manifestation of his true presence among us. This is why Clare is not satisfied with giving to Jesus the title "Christ" but it must be "the poor Christ." In her writings, we observe that the qualifier "poor" is simultaneously attributed to Christ and to humans. In taking the human condition, Christ becomes "the poor Christ" for the same reason as men and women, in their state as creatures, are "in utter poverty" (1 LAg 20). The "poor Christ" is God who became man. It is not a matter of seeking him beyond this world but rather of finding him in human beings, ourselves and others: to find Christ in men and women; in Christ, to see the Father; to see God in human beings, seeing what is great in what is small, the Creator in the creature—such is the extraordinary mystical intuition of Clare in her letters to Agnes of Prague. This "great Lord" who came to share our human condition is the God made man who took on the flesh of our fragile humanity. He chose to be born as an infant in a woman's womb! God is the infinitely Great, though with a greatness that was only translated into and expressed by poverty and humility. The Incarnation is humble poverty. God is poor in terms of a poverty that is humility. God's greatness is God's infinite poverty. God is all, God gives all and God has nothing.

Through his supreme *kenosis,* God is "King of heaven and earth." Therefore, we can only know God if we sustain the paradox of conceiving in the infinitely rich the infinite poverty of the One who loved us. The face of God is the face of a human being. The Incarnation of Christ expresses God's abasement. The only God, the transcendent One, the God who cannot be grasped, enters into what we consider the confinement, the smallness, of the human body. Clare uses contrasting words. In her writings, if we look at the different terms "King," "Son," "Lord," "Lamb," "Creator," "Eternal," we are amazed to discover the striking way in which Clare defines them:

—"The King" reigns in a stable: "The King of angels, / the Lord of heaven and earth, / is laid in a manger" (4 LAg 21).

—"[T]hough *more beautiful than the children of men*... [He] became, for your salvation, the lowest of men, was despised, struck, scourged untold times throughout His entire body, and then died amid the suffering of the Cross" (2 LAg 20). "The foxes have dens, He says, and the birds of the air have nests, but the Son of Man, Christ, has nowhere to lay His head... but bowing His head gave up His spirit" (1 LAg 18).

—"The Lord" is poor and needy: "O God-centered poverty, / whom the Lord Jesus Christ / Who ruled and now rules heaven and earth, / Who spoke and things were made, / condescended to embrace before all else!" (1 LAg 17). He is "so great and good a Lord, then, on coming into the virgin's womb, [he] chose to appear despised, needy, and poor in this world" (1 LAg 19).

—*"[T]he spotless Lamb,"* the one whose beauty is constantly admired by the blessed hosts of heaven, is *"the splendor of eternal glory," "the brilliance of eternal light and the mirror without blemish."* In this mirror, "blessed poverty, holy humility and inexpressible charity" are reflected (4 LAg 8, 10, 14, 15, 18).

—The Creator, "Who spoke and things were made," came "into the Virgin's womb" (1 LAg 17, 19). A Son "whom the heavens could not contain" the Virgin "carried . . . in the little enclosure of her holy womb" (3 LAg 18, 19). "[T]he most worthy of all creatures," the soul of faithful people, "is greater than heaven itself, since the heavens and the rest of creation cannot contain their Creator and only the faithful soul is His dwelling place and throne" (3 LAg 21–22).

—"The eternal King" chose to die! "[T]he Lamb, the eternal King . . . the King of all ages" chose "to suffer on the wood of the Cross and to die there the most shameful kind of death" (4 LAg 1, 4, 22).

Clare goes beyond the amazingly simple statement that God took on the human form and condition. For her, in his Incarnation, Christ not only identified with the poorest of humans but also became the most despised of them. This mystery of God is disconcerting. Preferring contempt to honors, the Lord Jesus Christ "did not regard equality with God as something to be exploited" (Philippians 2:6). He preferred to be poor and despised in the world, like an insignificant being. We must keep returning to this mystery. Why did God manifest himself in this manner? This mystery is incomprehensible to those who expect God to manifest himself in power. God chose to appear scorned, needy and poor.

### *An Inexplicable Face*

The glory of God shines on the face of the poor Christ. In "poor and humble Jesus Christ" (3 LAg 4), God took on a face"and his face was like the sun shining with full force" (Revelation 1:16). No one had ever seen the face of God but it was shown in Christ (John 1:18). The poor Christ is the perfect mirror of the Father, "the mirror without blemish," the manifestation of transcendence in immanence, of the invisible in the visible. Christ is the splendor of the "eternal glory" of his Father, "the brilliance of eternal light." The mirror is linked to the image. All God's eternity is concentrated and reflected in Christ, the mirror. Christ reflects the light. He shines with splendor. Jesus is "the mirror of eternity," the perfect image of the invisible God. Christ is the face of the divine substance. The wish that guided Clare during all her life was to have us discern this face of Christ in the same way we discern an image in a mirror. When we hold a mirror up to the sun, although we do not focus on the sky, we still see the sun clearly. The face of the Father shows through in the mirror of Christ: "No one has ever seen God. It is God the only Son, who is close to the Father's heart, who has made him known" (John 1:18).

Clare of Assisi invites us to enter into the tremendous adventure of discovering the splendor of God in the total weakness of Christ. For Clare, only this marvelous mystery could bring forth a constantly renewed source of life, light and love. She certainly discerned the features of divine beauty on the face of the poor Christ. And every time she returned to the contemplation of that face, she experienced the same joy. The happiness that she lived was so great that she felt the desire to write of her spiritual experience to Agnes.

### *The Paradox of Marred Beauty*

The experience of beauty on the face of the poor Christ is the experience of the otherness of God. In his Passion, Christ was neither handsome nor attractive. "He was oppressed and he was afflicted, / yet he did not open his mouth; / like a lamb that is led to the slaughter, / and like a sheep that before its shearers is silent, / so he did not open his mouth" (Isaiah 53:7).

The most beautiful of the children of men, Christ whose face shines like the sun, allowed himself to be disfigured, crucified and laid in a tomb. Clare's thought consists precisely in plunging into that beauty, into the greatest depth of what God reveals about God.

How are we to understand this paradox of marred beauty? What is the origin of Clare's attraction to the poor Christ? What is the beauty that characterizes Christ in such a way that, for Clare, his marred face is seen as supreme beauty? The answer seems evident to her: the cross says all there is to say about love and love contains its own evidence if it is true, according to Christ's own words, that "No one has greater love than this, to lay down one's life for one's friends" (John 15:13). For Clare, the entire movement of God's abasement in Christ is a movement of love. The real manifestation of the cross of Christ ends in the mystery of God's union with the world. The origin of this union between God and the world is found in Christ in whom supreme love is achieved. The poverty of the cross is the revelation of the heart of God because God can be seen in the mirror of Jesus' life, death and resurrection. This extreme darkness on the face of the poor Christ becomes precisely the supreme expression of God: the heart of God is unveiled in the heart of the poor Christ. Everything about God is said there. In his humanity, Christ manifests before our eyes the mysterious love of God who did not create evil or death.[6] The darkened face of Christ is transfigured with beauty by the threefold mystery of humility, poverty and love. God is revealed in the features of the poor Christ. This is the abasement and the condescension of love. Such a love transforms humanity from within. What we call the sacred is overturned: human life is capable of becoming divine. God is no longer separated from humankind. Jesus is the only indispensable mirror that enables us to discover and to recognize God. In Jesus, we are led to the Father. Jesus is "the Way, and the Truth, and the Life" (John 14:6). Recognition of this may be the most profound movement and the most outstanding aspect of Clare's theological and spiritual experience.

In Clare, the experience of beauty is situated at the crossroads of love and poverty. In the encounter of love, Christ is welcomed for himself as someone who is very close to us, yet, at the same time, very different from us. He is the Other. Because of that, even his face of poverty resists, fulfills and captivates us. This experience of Otherness is the experience of the mystery of God as God is. This face is truly inexplicable and this is precisely what makes it so attractive.

## *Notes*

[1] References to the term "Christ" in Clare's Writings: 1 LAg 28, 31; 3 LAg 1, 2, 11; 4 LAg 2, 7, 37; RCl 1, 3; TCl 48, 57, 59; BCl 6.

[2] The root of the term "Christ" (*Christos*) comes from the Greek word *chriô,* meaning "to anoint."

[3] "Lord" is the royal title of *Yahweh,* whose name, expressed by the sacred tetragrammaton, was transposed into *Adonai*: "My Lord." It signifies the confidence of servants in his absolute sovereignty. At times, this title was used almost as the proper name for God. In Greek it is *Kyrios,* which sometimes stands for "the incommunicable name of God."

Starting with Psalm 110, Jesus shows that the Messiah is "Lord," and therefore superior to David, whose son he is. The early Christians saw Jesus as the Lord (Acts 2:36; Romans 10:9; 1 Corinthians 12:3, etc.), which does not refer to the nature of Jesus Christ but to his power: he is attributed the same sovereignty as *Yahweh* (X. Léon-Dufour, "Seigneur," *Dictionnaire du Nouveau Testament* [in English, *Dictionary of the New Testament*, Terrence Prendergast, trans. New York: Harper & Row, 1980], p. 489). Following are the references of the word *Lord* in Clare's Writings: 1 LAg 3, 19, 25, 33, 35; 2 LAg 14, 15, 25; 3 LAg 4, 10, 33, 40, 41, 42; 4 LAg 38; RCl 3, 14; 8, 2, 3; 9, 4, 7, 8, 9; 10, 6, 12.

[4] "In Revelation, the risen Christ is presented in the figure of a lamb (Greek: *arnion*) that had been slaughtered (Rev 5:6–12; 13:8) but was alive and glorious (Rev 5:8, 13; 14:1). He is leading the fight and liberates God's people with a lion's power. This image comes from apocalyptic literature (Henoch) who puts a lamb instead of a strong beast at the head of the flock. The Lamb is the master of history and he invites humans to follow him (Rev 7:17; 14:4; 15:3) until the marriage of the Lamb (Rev 19:7, 9; 21:9). John presents Jesus as the Lamb (Greek: *amnos*) who takes away the sin of the world (Jn 1:29). This presentation is part of the apocalyptic tradition of the victorious Lamb [. . . ] who purifies the world from its sin (1 Jn 3:4 ff.)" (*Ibid.*, "Lamb of God"), p. 103.

[5] 4 LAg 14; ECl p. 113: "*quae cum sit splendor aeternae gloriae* (for he is the splendor of eternal glory)." The feminine expression *quae* is used. It is referring to Christ's Beauty (see 4 LAg 10).

[6] "[B]ecause God did not make death, / and he does not delight in the death of the living" (Wisdom 1:13).

# Conclusion

We have looked briefly at the life of Clare of Assisi and the evolution of her Order. We have also undertaken a close reading of Clare's correspondence with Agnes of Prague.

We began with a reflection on the human condition. In fact, in her letters to Agnes, Clare emphasizes our need as human beings to discover our real desire by recognizing the limitations of our condition and the call, inscribed in the depths of our being, to enter into the marvelous exchange of the humanity of God in Jesus Christ and our own humanity.

Part Two of this book looked at the notions of poverty, humility and charity as they are manifested in Jesus' life. Christ was seen as the crucified Lamb in whose weakness he is paradoxically revealed to be the glorious King of all creatures. Poverty, humility and charity are the border, surface and depth of a "mirror without blemish," the face of Jesus Christ that opens up a transformation to the divine for those who know how to set their eyes on him. The beauty of Jesus' face is at the crossroads of love and poverty.

Taking up Clare's commentary on the Song of Solomon, the remainder of the book analyzed the varying degrees of this transformation from the world to the divine, from the consideration of the poor Christ, to the union of heart, spirit and body with him and in him. Conforming to Christ means allowing ourselves to be transformed "in the image of his divinity." That was Clare's life and it was a luminous life.

If this work, as a whole, seemed to move from the historical to the mystical, it is because we have sought to present an introduction to Clare of Assisi's life and spirituality. We could not bypass a few historical highlights before coming to the heart of the matter.

In addition, in this book, only Clare's letters to Agnes of Prague have been abundantly quoted and commented upon. What about the content of Clare's other writings, briefly presented in the Introduction? It is true that a careful and comparative study of these texts has to be continued. Only after that will we be able to present a comprehensive view of Clare's theology based on her writings. However, among all the texts that have been preserved, Clare's letters to Agnes appear to reveal most about her experience and thought. The three types of writings (Testament, Rule and letters) are, in fact, oriented toward particular themes: the assertion of fidelity (Testament and chapter 6 of the Rule), the organization of community life (Rule) and her spiritual experience (letters).

## *The Content of the Letters*

Readers who came to this book with only an anecdotal knowledge of Clare will have been surprised by the rich content of her correspondence. Throughout her letters to Agnes, Clare proposes a close union between human beings and God. In the course of this book, we have attempted to do justice to the originality of Clare's thought in its twofold dimension. Clare's fundamental experience is the experience of the Christic nuptial union, close to the spiritual currents of her day marked by Saint Bernard and his movement.

Clare's intelligence is the intelligence of the perception, contemplation and the welcoming of the mystery of God in human mystery. By contemplating God made man, Clare is welcoming the reality of the Incarnation. The Incarnation is not an abstraction for her. The Incarnation is

Someone who really does exist: the poor Christ whom we contemplate under the different aspects of the mystery of his human and divine life.

### *The Humanity of Christ*

Clare expresses with great ease her feelings toward the humanity of Christ. Her imagination plays an important role in this meditation: she practices the composition of place[1] by reenacting in her mind the circumstances under which the different events of Christ's life took place.

Christ's infancy offers the possibility of adopting an attitude of poverty and humility by imitating the virtues of the God-Man. Here all the feeling Clare is capable of is integrated into the love she has for God having become a small child.

In all the scenes of the Passion and death of Christ, Clare takes part in the Lord's suffering while firmly believing in his Resurrection. The most shameful death possible, his death on the cross, is a sorrowful and glorious mystery. It is the harbinger of his Resurrection. Jesus' death is the act of his glorification and the pledge of our own.

### *Balanced Theological Thought*

Clare's thinking is characterized by the balance she always kept regarding all the aspects of the mystery of Christ that manifest his divinity and his humanity, his glory and his deliberate abasement. This theological balance is evident in all Clare's writings. This balance is an element of her thinking that is contrary to certain periods of history during which Christ is almost exclusively shown in the sorrowful moments of his human life and depicted with the face and the body of a tortured man. In Clare, this balance is a well-grounded theological value.

## *Being Transformed in Christ*

In Clare's mind, devotion to the humanity of Christ goes hand in hand with an ongoing effort to walk in his footsteps, to follow him and to imitate him (2 LAg 20; TCl 56). The imitation of Christ is a participation in his mystery. This is expressed in precise terms: Jesus is the "form," the model that contains all the reality of our salvation. At the beginning of her Rule (RCl 1, 1–2), Clare wrote "The form of life of the Order of the Poor Sisters . . . is this: to observe the Holy Gospel of our Lord Jesus Christ." What is at stake here for the sisters is to allow the teachings of Christ to "form" them so that they could be "transformed" in his image. Jesus is the gospel in person. He was and he remains the "spiritual form." To "conform ourselves" to him is to be "transformed" in his image and likeness. That implies a whole process of conversion and sanctification that makes it possible to live in Christ. "Place your mind before the mirror of eternity! / Place your soul *in the brilliance of glory*, / Place your heart *in the figure of the* divine *substance*! / And *transform* your entire being *into the image* / of the Godhead Itself through contemplation" (3 LAg 12–13).

## *Discovering the Name of God*

In the poor Christ, God has become for us the Face so that all human beings might discover their own faces in him. The human face of God is inexhaustible and all the more amazing because it is manifested in poverty and humility. In order for Clare to discover God's name, she needed this long fidelity to the Unimaginable in patience and in faith, in the long exodus of the days and nights of her existence. The face of the poor Christ reveals Someone else, a reality that we cannot analyze, classify or completely understand because it is always beyond us and strangely absent when we attempt to grasp it. Until her death, Clare opened up to the inexhaustible discovery of that face, light and origin, in the darkness and expectation of the eternal sun:

> But since the Lord was very near and, as it were, already standing at the door, she wished the priests and her spiritual brothers to stand by and read the Passion of the Lord and holy words. When Brother Juniper appeared among them, that excellent jester of the Lord who uttered the Lord's words which were often warming, she was filled with a new joy and asked him if he had had anything new from the Lord. When he opened his mouth, he burst forth with words that were like burning sparks coming from the furnace of his fervent heart. The virgin of the Lord took great comfort in his parables . . . . But the most holy virgin, turning towards herself, silently addressed her soul. "Go without anxiety," she said, "for you have a good escort for your journey. Go," she said, "for He Who created you has made you holy. And, always protecting you as a mother her child, He has loved you with a tender love. May you be blessed, O Lord," she said, "You Who have created my soul!"[2]

## *Notes*

[1] This is an element of prayer that consists in using the imagination to visualize the place where the event that is the object of meditation unfolded.

[2] Thomas of Celano, "The Legend of Saint Clare," Part I, 45–46, ED, pp. 295–296.

# Bibliography

*The asterisk (*) preceding an entry denotes a work added to the English translation.*


Bartoli, Marco. *Claire d'Assise*. Paris: Arthème Fayard Publication, 1993.

*Bartoli, Marco. *Clare of Assisi*. Sister Frances Teresa, trans. Quincy, Ill.: Franciscan Press, 1993.

"Bull of Canonization" of Saint Clare of Assisi in D. Vorreux (ed.), *Sainte Claire d'Assise. Documents.*

*"Bull of Canonization" of Saint Clare of Assisi in *Clare of Assisi: Early Documents.*

Camus, Albert. *L'Homme révolté.* Paris: Gallimard, coll. "Idées," 1951.

*Camus, Albert. *The Rebel: An Essay on Man in Revolt*, Anthony Bower, trans. New York: Vintage Books, 1991.

Claire d'Assise. *Ecrits*, Paris: Editions du Cerf, coll. "Sources chrétiennes," no. 325, 1985.

**Clare of Assisi: Early Documents*. Regis J. Armstrong, O.F.M. CAP., ed., trans. Saint Bonaventure, N.Y.: Franciscan Institute Publications, 1993.

Exupère de Prats-de-Mollo, O.F.M. CAP. *L'Esprit de sainte Claire*. Paris: Casterman, 1912.

**Francis of Assisi: Early Documents, 3 Volumes*, Regis J. Armstrong, O.F.M. CAP., J.A. Wayne Hellmann, O.F.M. CONV., William J. Short, O.F.M., eds. New York: New City Press, 1999-2001.

François d'Assise, *Ecrits*. Paris: Editions du Cerf, coll. "Sources chrétiennes," no. 285, 1981.

Leclerc, Eloi. *François d'Assise, le retour à l'Evangile*. Paris: Desclée de Brouwer, 1981.

*Leclerc, Eloi. *Francis of Assisi: Return to the Gospel*. Chicago: Franciscan Herald Press, 1983.

Léon-Dufour, Xavier. *Dictionnaire du Nouveau Testament*. Paris: Editions du Seuil, coll. "Parole de Dieu," 1975.

*Léon-Dufour, Xavier. *Dictionary of the New Testament*, Terrence Prendergast, trans. New York: Harper & Row, 1980.

Marie Colette, Sister (A Poor Clare of Nice). *Regard sur l'histoire des Clarisses*, privately published—*pro manuscripto*—text reproduced by the Poor Clares of Paray-le-Monial, 1979.

"Process of canonization" of Saint Clare of Assisi in D. Vorreux, ed., *Sainte Claire d'Assise. Documents*.

*Process of Canonization" of Saint Clare of Assisi in *Clare of Assisi: Early Documents*.

Purfield, Brian E. *Reflets dans le miroir (Images du Christ dans la vie spirituelle de sainte Claire d'Assise)*. Paris: Editions franciscaines, 1993.

*Purfield, Brian E. *Reflections in the Mirror: The Images of Christ in the Spiritual Life of Saint Clare of Assisi*. M.A. Thesis, St. Bonaventure University, 1989.

Rahner, Karl. "*La doctrine des sens spirituals au Moyen Age (en particulier chez Saint Bonaventure,*" *Revue d'ascétique et de mystique*, July 1933.

*Rahner, Karl, "The Doctrine of the 'Spiritual Senses' in the Middle Ages (especially in St. Bonaventure)," *Theological Investigations*, Vol. XVI, pp. 263–299.

*Redemptor hominis*, Encyclical Letter, 1979.

"*Sacrum commercium*," in T. Desbonnets and D. Vorreux, eds., *Saint François d'Assise. Documents.*

*"*Sacrum commercium*," in *Francis of Assisi: Early Documents.*

*Sainte Claire d'Assise. Documents*, Damien Vorreux, ed. Paris: Editions franciscaines, 1983.

Saint-Exupéry, Antoine de. *Le Petit Prince.* Paris: Gallimard, 1975.

*Saint-Exupéry, Antoine de. *The Little Prince*, Katherine Woods, trans. San Diego: Harcourt Brace & Co., 1993.

*Saint François d'Assise. Documents.* Théophile Desbonnets and Damien Vorreux, eds. Paris: Editions franciscaines, 1981.

Thomas of Celano, "Vie de sainte Claire d'Assise," in D. Vorreux, ed., *Sainte Claire d'Assise. Documents.*

*Thomas of Celano, "The Legend of Saint Clare," in *Clare of Assisi: Early Documents.*

Thomas of Celano, "Vita prima," in T. Desbonnets and D. Vorreux, eds., *Saint François d'Assise. Documents.*

*Thomas of Celano, "The Life of Saint Francis," in *Francis of Assisi: Early Documents.*

Tourenne, Yves. "*L'admirable échange*," *Claire dans nos fédérations, Bulletin of the Federations of Poor Clares*, no. 24, Easter 1995.